Mystical Experiences

A Memoir of My Spiritual Unfoldment

David Wattam

Published by Eternal Swan Publishing

Contact: eternal.swan.publishing@gmail.com

A catalogue record for this book is available from the National Library of New Zealand.

ISBN 978-0-473-62577-1 (paperback)

ISBN 978-0-473-62578-8 (EPUB)

Picture credits: All photographs collection of the author.

Contents

‘I don’t believe it,’ said Luke Skywalker.

‘And that is why you fail,’ responded Yoda.

—*Star Wars: Episode V – The Empire Strikes Back*

Prologue

Is there a source of universal justice and truth? I always had an inner urge to find out. This yearning dominated much of my life. Does it seem logical that spiritual truth was accessible only to devout geniuses of the distant past? I eventually had experiences that confirm that access to genuine truth, not just opinion, can be achieved. Did I need to find a teacher? Just maybe a teacher who 'knows' would find me. I empathise with Ralph Waldo Emerson who said, 'I hate quotations. Tell me what you know.'

My hope that I may be 'led' to teachers that are alive now eventually came true, but there was a long delay because I had to first endure the consequences of taking a wrong turning. You need to be prepared to believe the most impossible things that happen more often than most people are aware of. Keeping an open mind is essential.

Chapter 1
My early years

When I was a child, what had stirred up my interest in having an invisible being as a counsellor and patient friend? I do not remember having heard of God or Jesus until I was about seven years old. When I was four years old and my father owned a farm near Cambridge, my mother ran off with the farm worker, taking me with them, leaving behind three older siblings. They were devastated. Mum's father guessed where she was, and he had convinced her to return with me to rejoin my siblings. She left again three weeks later but remained in touch with Dad and her children.

My father must have thought that I should know something about religion, so he sent me to the local Sunday school in a nearby country hall. I remember being impressed by a beautifully dressed young girl reading a heart-warming story about a person named Jesus. He sounded like a wonderful man who cared about people. He had advice from an invisible being called God. It was very disappointing for me to see the sweet girl was not so sweet when the story-telling period was over, and the other children present, who were also dressed in their best clothes, were not all kind and considerate after the reading had finished. Why were they disregarding the lessons that Jesus had taught? I was puzzled and disappointed and did not want to return to Sunday school, but I felt relieved that I now had been told about a wise counsellor that I could tell all my troubles to: God. The meagre information that I had heard gave me a basic philosophy — there was a being that knew about my loneliness and despair. I had been feeling desperate and completely unable to communicate my feelings to anyone, but by talking to God I got the strength to get past the sickening dread that I felt about being in a hopeless situation: I missed the love of my mother but felt loyal to my father and siblings. One of the topics that I talked to God about was: why are some people unkind, inconsiderate, and dishonest? Why had I been left motherless? I did not have any resentment towards my mother and wanted to avoid hearing any criticism of her. I was frightened that I would collapse into a panicking mess if I tried to discuss my despair. Other children at school appeared to have been supervised before being sent to school with handkerchiefs, good food and necessary equipment such as sharpened pencils. I always felt as if school mornings were a mad scramble to find my clothes from a large pile of laundry. I would have felt more valued if I had had more considerate assistance — even to get dressed.

I remember having a brief lunch with my mother several years later, but I could not hug her or tell her that I missed her. I might not have been able to not cry and then Mum would have told my father that I wanted to live with her, and I would have felt disloyal if my father misunderstood and thought that I did not appreciate him. However, over the following years I had extended visits with her. I could never have a frank talk with either my father nor my mother; it might have dredged up the bleak feeling of dread. I really wanted heartfelt communication — to be understood. I have since retained an inability, a weakness, to query any person in authority why they make the decisions they do. It did not help that I had 'the strap' — punished — at school, for something that I did not do when I was about eight years old. I was not capable of giving a statement in my defence. Our housekeeper's daughter bullied me at school and Dad never knew. Even in my mature years I am reluctant to ask probing questions of anyone or complain to anyone about perceived injustices. Unfair behaviour should be obvious to the perpetrator.

During my life I made an endeavour to always stay honest. Although I rarely attended a church, I retained a basic belief that there must be an indescribable non-human intelligence regulating all the universes. The God of my childhood was a sympathetic recording system that may possibly be able to influence the course of events.

In my teen years I read about people who have some sort of psychic perception — called extrasensory perception, or ESP, since the 1930s by the Duke Parapsychology Laboratory of Duke University, North Carolina. I wanted to train myself to have only positive thoughts because that may be a way to clear my mind of negative emotions, and then some sort of clairvoyant or telepathic ability may develop. All these ideas were very vague with no clear way forward identified about how to develop them. When I was twelve years old, I noticed that there was a cloudiness about my thinking; the cloudiness must be caused by my emotions, so I tried to reduce the amount of time re-enacting negative experiences, including recent ones. I did not want to blame anyone for their apparent lack of judgment.

A cry for help answered

A turbulent period of my life started when I was 22 years old, in 1962. My older brother and I worked in my father's furniture and curtain shop in Devonport on Auckland's North Shore. I shared a flat with a young married couple in Takapuna, five kilometres from Devonport near a Harbour Bridge approach road.

One Friday evening I went to a local dance and met a 20-year-old woman named Mary. I felt an instant attraction to her, and immediately felt as if I had found my ideal partner. On the following Sunday, I visited her; she was renting a room from a young couple with a baby who lived near the Mt Eden shops across the Harbour Bridge.

Mary told me that she had suffered from recurring headaches in the past, and she had not been going to work in a telephone exchange since the pains had increased the week before. I visited her several times over the next three weeks, and we went to the movies twice. I had become infatuated with her, but I was also feeling anxious about her inability to earn a living and her apparent lack of a plan on how to survive financially, and because she did not appear to be doing anything constructive at home. I assumed that she must have had some savings. I felt apprehensive; I may be getting involved in a situation that I have not had any experience about — what decisions need to be made? After all, I hardly knew her. Who was going to be responsible for her welfare?

One month after meeting her, on a Saturday evening, Mary and I were babysitting while the young couple went to the local movie theatre. Mary started to get a headache about half past eight, so she went to her room to lie down. Within half an hour she was complaining: 'All the bones in my head are starting to ache!' Mary told me that she had already taken the medication that her doctor had prescribed. A few minutes later she said she was in agony, and she clutched her head. I was very worried and so I decided to phone for an ambulance and then I rang the movie theatre to request them to put a message on the screen to get the baby's parents to come home, and 20 minutes later they arrived. When the ambulance came the officers decided to take Mary to Auckland Hospital, and I was so worried that I went in the ambulance with her. Mary was admitted as a patient and remained there for five days. The doctors had not been able to find out what was causing the headaches, but an appointment with a neurologist in three weeks' time was made for her. I was feeling relieved when I visited her to see her laughing and joking with the staff because she appeared to have recovered.

I took Mary to Takapuna the following Saturday and introduced her to my flatmates. All went well at first, but within half an hour Mary had become semi-conscious after rapidly getting an extreme headache. She was taken away in an ambulance again, but she was soon sent home — she had the appointment with the neurologist still to come.

The following Sunday I was in Mt Eden visiting Mary again; she appeared to be tired and listless. During the evening, some people from an adjacent flat came to visit because they had heard about Mary's unusual condition and seemed concerned about her welfare. What might be done to solve her problem? About eight o'clock Mary went to her room to lie down because her headache had returned, although she had been continuing to take the medication approved by the doctors at the hospital, and so I was not unduly worried. However, I started to despair when she became semi-conscious and started mumbling softly with her eyes closed; I felt helpless, because there seemed little point in calling an ambulance again. When I listened carefully to her subdued whispers, she was repeatedly complaining about head pains, and then she started to panic and cry out: 'The bones in my head are aching!' She appeared to have become delirious and was not actually talking specifically to me. She started thrashing around, and in a loud desperate voice, said: 'I want to marry David now! Get a minister now!' She was obviously not fully conscious — her eyes were still closed. For several minutes she continued to implore someone to respond to her, but then she became silent and appeared to be in a disturbed sleep. I was distraught. Some neighbours visiting had witnessed what was happening because the bedroom door to the lounge was open.

I was panicking. There did not seem to be any solution to this crisis. One of the visitors was a confident-looking young woman. She told me: 'Recently I wanted to commit suicide. I consulted a brilliant young psychologist who convinced me not to kill myself. I want an excuse to see him now — I could phone him and tell him about Mary and ask him to come; then I will be able to see him too.' Although she had a selfish motive, I thought that her idea was worth trying, although I was almost certain that a professional psychologist was unlikely to make house calls. I told the girl to make the call, but would psychology be of any use if Mary has a physical or nervous malfunction? A few minutes later the girl was excitedly shrieking: 'Doctor Rickard is going to come!' Several more neighbours turned up to see what was going to happen.

Thirty minutes later I heard a car driving up the steep driveway, then as the doorbell rang, I heard a dull thump — somehow Mary's tossing about had caused her to fall out of bed. As I was lifting her back onto her bed a man's commanding voice said: 'Leave her alone!' A tall man who was about 36 years old had entered the room accompanied by an attractive woman about 22 years old. The man asked for someone to bring three chairs, and they were promptly brought. There were now about six concerned people crowding into the bedroom. 'Everybody out! Shut the door!' said Dr Rickard emphatically. The onlookers looked disappointed but left and closed the door.

'What is her name?' asked the doctor. After he was told, he sat near Mary and said in a firm voice, 'Hello, Mary.' Mary stirred. 'Mary! Wake up!' said the doctor loudly. Mary moved sluggishly. 'Wake up, Mary!' said the doctor again, in a commanding voice. Mary, in a voice that was very slurred, said, 'Who's that?'

'Mickey Mouse!' responded the doctor. Mary now appeared to be semi-conscious, but her eyes were still closed. She giggled. 'Who are you really?'

'My friends call me Max — you can call me Max,' he said. 'I am here to help you.'

A minute passed before Mary opened her eyes and was able to speak softly. She did not complain any more about a headache, but she looked exhausted. During the next hour, she told Max that her father had divorced her mother and remarried. When she was younger, Mary and her Catholic stepmother had clashed, but Mary loved her father. Mary was sent away to a supervised facility for troubled young people. She told Max that she had a brother who lived in Nelson and she had not seen him for years.

Max did not discuss Mary's problem all the time. He talked about how his methods were unconventional, so he was unpopular with some psychologists and patients, but he got quick genuine results. He was going to shake up his profession and wake this country up to some of society's problems. 'People will never forget my name,' he said. He gave me the impression that he really believed he had the ability to achieve health and society reforms. In the future I was to hear him repeat these emphatic statements many times when he first met anyone.

Max told me not to go home this evening because Mary was very intuitive and would know if I had left. He suggested that I ask for permission to sleep on a couch there, and in the morning bring Mary to consult him at his clinic in the city at nine o'clock — his clinic was ten minutes' drive away from here. He and his assistant, Adrienne, left about ten o'clock. I was to learn that Max had challenged her earlier that evening. She had offered to be his secretary and endeavour to collect the many unpaid professional fees and do his office work, because financially he was struggling. Max had said to Adrienne, 'If the phone rang now and someone was urgently needing help, would you be willing to go with me and attend to them?' As Adrienne responded 'Yes', Max's patient had rung to ask him to help Mary.

I slept well on a couch. I was woken up by Mary's bubbly laughing at eight o'clock, but within half an hour she had to be assisted to finish dressing and was barely able to stand or speak. It took two people to support her to walk to my car and get in.

At Max's clinic we all sat in comfortable armchairs — Mary was barely conscious. Within a few minutes she had passed out. Max stood up, said, 'Damned drugs!' and looking at me, said, 'Tell Mary you love her. Tell her in a way that she knows you really mean it.' I felt helpless; the words would not come out of my mouth. Somehow, I could not say anything. Max moved quickly to stand in front of Mary. 'Mary! Stand up!' he commanded. He repeated the command, and Mary, who still had not opened her eyes, stood up, and suddenly she burst into tears and threw her arms around Max. 'Just think of me as your big brother,' said Max. 'No — father,' said Mary as she opened her eyes and sobbed. Max then told her that he had a lot of patients around New Zealand who were like his daughters. At Max's suggestion we made individual appointments for the following week for Mary and me.

The next time I saw Mary, she told me that Max had advised her to travel to Nelson to meet up with her estranged brother, but she should not stay longer than 10 days. When I kept my appointment with Max, he invited his wife, an attractive blonde, to sit in with us. My heart sank when she appeared to be uninterested in paying attention. Max dismissed her after 10 minutes. He spent time looking at fish in his fish tank and wondered what they thought about. He talked about reincarnation. Where were all the questions that the TV psychologists asked? He asked me if I ever got angry. I told him that it was rare for me. I considered that there was a deep soul behind the personality, the personality that had done wrong, and I would forgive their outer faults. The real soul would be untarnished and hopefully influencing the personality. He asked me bluntly, 'Do you masturbate?' I had probably misheard him and so I replied that my chewing was fine. Max laughed. He asked me what I wanted to do with my life. 'I want to do something to help people,' I told him, feeling very self-conscious. He invited me to attend a lecture that he gave every Monday night at his clinic for patients that had told him they wanted to help people.

On the following Monday, I was listening to him speak to an audience of 28 people. I was inspired by his words — he said that our minds are powerful and can achieve wonders. One of the men present had been on a fast for three weeks and it was not obvious which man that was. This information enthused me so much that I immediately started a week-long fast. I drank a lot of water, about one glass every hour or two, and never felt hungry. The following weekend I was digging drains for a holiday home owned by one of Max's students. When I weighed myself after six days, I had lost only three pounds. My belief that I could fast successfully led to success. To remain physically strong, I had to gradually start to eat on that Sunday afternoon — half a tinned pear felt like a rock in my stomach. However, I would fail whenever I attempted to fast in later years.

Mary surprised me by immediately arranging to travel to see her brother in Nelson. Within a week she was there and writing me pages of happy love letters every day. She had obviously ignored Max's advice, because she stayed in Nelson for three weeks. On the day that she arrived back in Auckland I was at the airport to welcome her back. I was so emotional that my heart was racing, so I checked my pulse. I counted 135 beats per minute — it was usually between 55 and 66. I felt very uneasy when Mary did not rejoice at our reunion when I greeted her, and she ignored my attempt to hug her. I felt a sense of dread — what had happened to cause her to greet me in an unemotional, lifeless manner?

She kept one last appointment with Max that had been arranged before she went to Nelson. When I visited her, she complained that she did not agree with what Max was telling her. I had no idea what that could be. Within about two weeks she had told me she did not love me any more and did not want to keep seeing me. Max did not give me any reason for the sudden change in Mary's feelings, but he advised me to see Mary again and ask her if she was certain that she did not want to see me again. I followed his advice and contacted Mary again, and she agreed to meet me. It was then that she sheepishly told me that she loved another man that I remembered seeing visiting just once before she left to travel to Nelson. I have often wondered what had caused her sudden change of heart.

Max told me that when Mary appeared to be unconscious, she had been aware that everyone was worried about her, but when he had arrived and spoken to her the first time, she could tell that he was not worried. She regained consciousness because in her subconscious she was curious to see if he could help her.

She had received an account from Max but did not see why she should pay it; what had he done for her? I was incredulous, because I felt that we had found a wise mentor in Max, and Mary had certainly been in want of a solution for her debilitating psychological problem. I never saw Mary again, and do not know whether she continued to have headaches.

The United People's Organisation

Max always talked and acted as if he was determined to do something positive to improve the health systems of New Zealand, and he was not going to put up with anyone obstructing him; he was going to shake things up. He took every opportunity to talk about how most of his patients had not been successfully treated by conventional professionals; they had been stuffed with drugs or given shock treatment. Eventually these people came to him as the last resort. He did not ask a lot of the questions of his patients that psychologists in the movies or on television usually asked, but he somehow got quick results. He mentioned that he was often unpaid — some of the patients who had consulted him were expecting him to continue to keep analysing them regularly like Freud, even when he considered that there was no need; he had promptly resolved the problem that they had consulted him about.

Adrienne became his unpaid secretary and debt collector and was soon to be his lover. Adrienne had briefly been married to a much older man who was a baker in Wellington. Max separated from his wife, probably around the time that I had met her, and they divorced about 18 months after these incidents.

Max appeared to be angry — he always used the word 'hot' — about how some authorities misused their power. He had been practising psychology in Wellington and owned a nightclub there. He said that he had ordered a police sergeant to leave his nightclub — the Starlight — because the sergeant was helping himself to excessive amounts of food in the kitchen. He seemed convinced that the Auckland police new about the incident and would cause trouble for him.

He had spent years formulating a plan that would bring to fruition his vision of organising a group of people who would staff a mental health facility for nervous disorders, an unmarried mothers' home, and an international orphanage. They also would conduct investigations into ESP and UFOs. He had created a charitable organisation named the United People's Organisation (Worldwide) Incorporated — UPO.

At one of the lectures, the audience was informed that there would be a meeting of UPO members, and I was present when there was an election of officers. Max was voted president, and Jack, a very chatty and peaceful-looking man who was a builder, was voted vice president. Was I officially a member? I voted, but I had not filled in a membership application form.

I had been relieved of responsibility for Mary's problems, but I sold my car to pay Max's accounts for each of us. I felt devastated for several weeks after Mary's decision, but I was sustained emotionally by the riveting lectures that Max was giving on Mondays, and the knowledge that he was succeeding with his plan to get people to support him and move ahead in forming UPO. I took notes of his lectures and I still have some of them. He talked about people having a consciousness and a super-consciousness connected to a higher cosmic source. He explained what an extrovert or introvert personality is. He said that one in 12 marriages end in divorce and it would be one in six before too long. Mental illness was also on the increase, and in a few years one person in six would be suffering. That did eventuate. Society was spiralling into disorder. UPO expected to provide harmonious living conditions and occupations for its members and appropriate treatment for people seeking counselling. He wanted to set an example, with the help of willing associates, of a mental health system that had positive results without the reliance on drugs as at present. I was excited to be hearing about subjects that had always been important to me. Max had stopped taking patients recently but some of his audience had already been counselled about their marriage troubles.

These experiences were the precursor to my becoming enthusiastic about joining Max and becoming one of his willing helpers to establish UPO and live with people that were of like mind. Max was my Robin Hood, my fighter for the ordinary person. Unfortunately, I had no natural predisposition or obvious talent for any occupation.

It was time to explain to my father what had been happening. I was not used to talking to him about emotional issues, so I had to force myself to tell him about my recent personal heartaches and my enthusiasm to join UPO. I hoped to have practical work to do that would be useful and satisfying. I knew that my father would probably think that Mary had had a mental problem and I was better off without her. I told him that I wanted to go and live with the UPO members in the city and help with the work that UPO would be doing to help people. Dad probably thought that I was too much of a dreamer. He never said a word to discourage me, so I stopped working for him three weeks later. I was afraid that he would not understand that I had a yearning for a lifestyle that in much later years I would call a spiritual one, one that took account of people's deeper yearning and needs.

Max invited me to move to a flat above his consulting rooms, which were now an office for UPO. My flatmates were two members who had paid jobs and donated their wages to UPO: Graeme, an intellectual 23-year-old man, and Margaret, a 26-

year-old woman who was often restless, impatient, and blunt speaking. It was necessary for all of us to work at paid jobs to help to meet UPO's expenses, and so I worked in grocers' shops for about 18 months. I felt grateful and loyal to Max for taking on Mary's case and having the knowledge to treat her. I had been in an emotional turmoil and now felt as if I was released from responsibility for her welfare. I was certain that Max had mastered mysterious ESP qualities and was not afraid of confidently laying ambitious plans for the future of UPO. He seemed determined to succeed. I considered him to be a dynamic wise man who would find a solution to every problem. Because of my loyalty I tended to overlook or forgive the errors he made and faults that became apparent during the oncoming years.

Rakino Island – UPO's home base

I had been surprised when I was told that UPO had bought Rakino Island in the Hauraki Gulf in 1963. The island was almost 2.4 kilometres long — about one and a half miles. It was 14 miles from central Auckland by launch — about 23 kilometres. The *New Zealand Herald* carried the news that suitable facilities would be established on the island by UPO for the treatment of mental disorders and other services. A large house, eventually known as The Lodge, and a smaller one nearby, sat near the beach in Home Bay on an area of flat land surrounded by low hills.

Transport to and from the island was provided by a 30-foot launch that had been included in the purchase price. Unfortunately, the jetty in Home Bay was not usable at low tide because the bay was too shallow.

The launch Rakino, *author pictured with Jack, Rosemary, and friend*

UPO had an agreement with a farmer to graze stock, and that continued for about four more years. Cattle were transported back and forth by barge; the farmer arrived periodically and stayed for two or three days at The Lodge. When I first set foot on Rakino I was puzzled — where were all the members that I had seen at the meeting to elect officers? The only other people present were Rosemary, Adrienne's 12-year-old sister, who would spend most of her time on Rakino and loved the farmer's horses, and Dorothy, the cook, who was a member of UPO.

I was surprised that a prominent advertisement, headed up 'Utopia', had been placed in the *New Zealand Herald*. It announced a public meeting to be held in the Princess Theatre in Auckland's main street to enlist members. One hundred people, who agreed with the society's aims and were seeking a rewarding lifestyle, were invited to join the society and donate their worldly goods. Two days after I was told about the upcoming meeting I sat with Max, Adrienne, and my flatmates in an empty theatre. We waited for an audience, but not one person arrived. As far as I know, the active members remained at seven for at least four years.

Sandy Bay, Rakino Island

I never knew who had provided the money to buy the island, and initially I did not know that there had been a mortgage still to pay. My two flatmates and myself and Max and Adrienne were not resident on Rakino all the time, because we worked in the city Monday to Friday because there was no permanent work for us on Rakino. The five of us lived on the city UPO rented premises. Three of us contributed our wages to UPO, and then Graeme and Margaret moved to Rakino sometime during 1964. I never kept any personal money for myself and presumed that my flatmates did not either. I never asked for money for envelopes or stamps to post birthday or Christmas cards and so I lost touch with my family over the next few years, and because I was not one to phone people regularly to keep in touch. Initially Max and Adrienne and us three flatmates travelled to Rakino on the launch on Saturday mornings with supplies, including gas bottles for cooking and diesel for the electricity generator, and returned Sunday afternoon. I would usually spend about eight hours mowing lawns around The Lodge.

I was amazed when Max announced that he was standing in the upcoming elections for Parliament in 1963 as a Social Credit candidate for Central Auckland. His photograph appeared in the New Zealand *Herald* with a brief biography. Margaret and I were with him when he went to two political campaign meetings in Jack's 1940 American pick-up truck. Max was introduced as Captain Ricketts at one meeting — the audience giggled when Max refused the honour. Max said that he did not want to be the Prime Minister, only the Minister of Health, but he was not elected.

In 1964, Sir Robert Kerridge, the owner of 133 movie theatres in New Zealand and Australia, had a meeting with Max. UPO had bought Rakino for 30,000 pounds — now Sir Robert offered to buy it for 60,000 pounds. Max told us that he had been nervous during the meeting and he had put his cigarette in his mouth back to front; he refused the offer. Sir Robert paid 80,000 pounds for another island nearby — Pakatoa Island — to develop it for a holiday resort. Max briefly told us that when he returned to New Zealand after the Second World

War was over, he reclaimed a job that he had had with Sir Robert prior to his joining the Air Force.

UPO's city coffee lounge

In 1964, I was told that a businessman had provided the finance for the construction of a coffee lounge that UPO was having built one minute's walk from the UPO office. Adrienne joked to me about how she had discreetly flirted with the man to help persuade him to help when she was with Max during a meeting. Adrienne was always excellent company and was never a wilting flower — but she could be domineering. Like with all Max's deals I was never told officially what was being planned. Early in 1964, I started working in The Australia Lounge and Gallery, the new coffee lounge. I had painted the interior until late at night after finishing my paid day job. Jack was a fastidious builder and had done a wonderful job of fitting out the premises that looked so bright and inviting that there was a queue waiting to enter on opening day. I was called over to wash dishes early in the morning. Max said he would ring my usual workplace and tell them I would not be back. I felt guilty for not giving my employer notice.

Max was often having discussions on the phone or in person with a lawyer or an accountant. In the first year of UPO I would often be present when he had long intense talks with Adrienne and so I had a glimpse of the problems facing him and what he was attempting to achieve, but I was never included. I purposely tried to avoid listening to the details of the conversations. I suspect that Jack was the only other member to be involved in any decision-making. Jack was very practical and a very honest man. I also know that us few other members were not executive material and Max obviously wanted to keep UPO problems on his own shoulders. Max was the president and I had no doubt that he was not going to kowtow to any UPO committee — if there had been one. Is that why most of the founding members had not continued to support Max?

When I asked Graeme how he had met Max, he told me that he had been a volunteer when Max had temporarily become 'The Great Ricardo' to perform a hypnotism show. I do not know why he had wanted to do the show, but Max only ever mentioned it once over the following years. Adrienne had also volunteered, and when hypnotised and told to help people in distress she had given them a cup of tea and said some comforting words. Adrienne told me that Max had later made her face her hysterical fear of spiders — the fear had never reoccurred. This led to her learning that Max's patients often did not pay for their consultations.

Adrienne had a lively strong personality, was an excellent organiser and supervisor and appeared to be an ideal secretary and sounding board for Max. She expected receipts from Max for every expense, even bus fares. She became the first manager of The Australia Lounge.

I heard discussions about Max's Wellington meeting with the Honourable Mr Shand, a government minister with whom he had quarrelled. I guessed that Max had pointed out he considered that under current law at that time Rakino Island was outside New Zealand's territorial waters and not subject to its laws, and therefore outside of the Auckland City Council's area of authority for matters like building consents, or health standards and roading. When Jack's truck was transported to Rakino, did it still need to comply with government laws?

Later in 1964, Max and Don — a man about Max's age who was a qualified hypnotherapist and who was a keen photographer and diver — and Don's friend Colin spent several weeks living on Motuihe Island 10 kilometres from Rakino. It had been a New Zealand Navy training base, but its functions had been moved to Narrow Neck on the North Shore in 1963. The buildings were being demolished and Max had negotiated with the contractor for some of the buildings. The demolition timber was transported by barge to Rakino. I remember spending weeks painting with a professional Australian painter who was an unpaid volunteer, and we painted a row of uncompleted rooms for accommodation that Jack had built alongside The Lodge. Jack had also constructed a shelter shed on Home Bay beach. A 65-year-old man, who looked like he had had a hard life but had handyman skills, had installed plumbing systems in the buildings from demolition materials. I do not know where he came from or how long he stayed but when I returned to Rakino after spending months in the city he was not there. I rarely asked questions about anything that happened. I was the private soldier who does not ask a general to explain. When some things had already happened, it seemed like there was no point in dissecting past events. I was always uncomfortable asking for explanations.

Our home, Rakino Island, is subdivided and a ferry service starts

At some time during 1964, Max called the members on Rakino to attend a meeting in the beach shelter shed that Jack had built. He had spent some weeks on Rakino obviously deep in thought and appeared to be trying to make some decisions. Everyone present at the meeting had grown to consider the island to be their home. Max announced that unfortunately, Rakino had to be subdivided. I probably misunderstood the implications — I thought that the money from the sale of sections after subdividing would be in UPO's charge to pay the mortgage.

The land was surveyed and roading contractors arrived in 1965 and spent over three months constructing roads, and a wharf in deep-water Sandy Bay, a 10-minute walk from The Lodge. Jack and I tramped up and down hills while he estimated where to place the advertising signs that identified where each section for sale was. I verified on Google in January 2020 that Rakino was subdivided, and a wharf constructed in 1965. At that time, I had thought that Max had negotiated with a roading contractor to receive land in exchange for constructing roads and a wharf; it is now obvious that I was mistaken. While writing this information I have been getting educated about some of the facts of UPO's financial situation at that time. I had not known that in 1964, because of UPOs financial problems, Rakino had been surrendered to the receivers, and it had then been bought by North Shore Ferries. Whether that sale included The Lodge and grounds I do not know. Max and Adrienne had briefly tried commercial fishing to raise money and for a few months paying guests had been catered for successfully at The Lodge. A television producer, Shirley Maddock, had visited and stayed one night at The Lodge, but I do not think that she was interested in presenting any of the aims of UPO to the viewers. I rowed a boat for the camera operator and later appeared on screen for about two seconds in the distance. Rakino Island was featured very briefly on the series Shirley produced, called 'Islands of the Gulf'.

Don and his friend Colin later used some of the demolition timber to construct basic houses on sections that I presumed they must have bought. I was getting used to finding out after the event about Max's decisions. Don and his girlfriend and Colin and his wife often stayed on Rakino. Except for Jack and Adrienne, the other members probably did not have any details about a mortgage and how it was going to be paid for. I had assumed that the successful coffee lounge of UPO's had been bringing enough income to pay the mortgage.

It is now obvious that I was mistaken. I have been learning what had not been fully explained by Max at the members' meeting on the beach. I was surprised to find that when I returned to Rakino after working in the city for months, Jack had built a large building to the rear of the recently constructed wharf for a refreshment rooms and shop, with an upstairs flat.

The road to the northern end of Rakino started from the wharf in picturesque Sandy Bay, a 10-minute walk from Home Bay. Tuatara was a small island opposite the wharf; it helped Sandy Bay provide a sheltered anchorage for boats and had deep water at low tide. Arthur, a charismatic 83-year-old gentleman from Remuera, owned a Second World War ex-torpedo boat; the original petrol motor had been replaced with a diesel engine. For several months during 1966, he had transported the city members and supplies to Rakino on Saturdays and stayed overnight on his vessel, returning the city dwellers to the city on Sundays. He had been the skipper for Sir James Wattie, the New Zealand millionaire canning factory magnate, who had bequeathed the craft to him. He had photographs of dining with the Shah of Iran. After Arthur had transported the members for several months, Max told me that he had argued with Arthur and he would not be transporting us to Rakino any more. Arthur had offered to buy Tuatara Island, and that had upset Max.

The North Shore Ferries started a regular service to Rakino on Saturdays but did not return until Sunday. Only the few section owners were aboard, and it was a big disappointment that there were no customers for the shop. I was expecting a few dozen sightseers, but I suppose that with no accommodation or camping area available and no same-day return ferry to Auckland, a trip to Rakino was impractical for most people. An amphibious seaplane landed in Sandy Bay occasionally, and Max's commanding officer from his Air Force days, former Squadron Leader Freddy Ladd — who later finished his career by flying his amphibious taxi plane under the Auckland Harbour Bridge – occasionally flew low over the large Lodge lawn and threw a rolled newspaper out a window with a brief cheery message scrawled on it. The regular ferry service was eventually cancelled. At some time when I was absent a Shell Oil diesel fuel pump had been installed on the wharf. The expected sales to boat owners did not eventuate, and the facility was removed. But who had been expected to man the diesel pump?

A scandal averted – or diverted

'Max had sex with me on the launch,' Margaret calmly told everyone who was gathered in The Lodge kitchen one evening, including Don. Max was expected to arrive from the city later. At first there was a shocked silence; nobody had been willing to discuss what had been said. Margaret seemed to be telling the truth. Should we believe her? She had been a rebel when she was young and had been forced to have shock treatment. She was now about 30 years old, and although she was often uncooperative and unsociable and sometimes complained that she should be paid, she was never belligerent. She had a habit of abruptly giving an honest response during a discussion that could be taken as rude or rebellious. Margaret's revelation was the biggest emotional upheaval that was ever to happen on Rakino. Everyone appeared to be stunned and alarmed — was Max less ethical than the image he portrayed? A few hours later when Max arrived in the launch from the city, he had immediately been told by Dorothy what had happened. Everyone else was conflicted and said nothing to him. About an hour later Max called everyone together and looked to be fuming, and when he spoke his voice was accusatory. He asked why everyone had not told him what Margaret had said. We may have all been feeling very ashamed because our responses inferred that perhaps we had believed Margaret.

The next day I walked into The Lodge lounge when Don, Jack, Margaret, and Max were there. I did not know what was being discussed, but Max suddenly became furious and lost his self-control. He suddenly screamed at Margaret — 'You bitch!' — and gave her two short punches to her chest. He was prevented from striking her again by Don. I had never seen Max furious before. It is only now as I write this that I am wondering if Adrienne, Dorothy the cook, and Graeme ever knew about that incident. I had assumed that they had known but they may never have been told about it. I do not know when Margaret left UPO, but it was probably late in 1966 when I was busy in the city for months at a time. During a conversation Max had casually mentioned that Margaret had a boyfriend.

It is difficult to describe the tension that often seemed to persist at times among the members that were on Rakino. Graeme had lived on Rakino since 1965. He appeared to feel as if he could not be of any practical use to UPO living there but he tried to keep a positive attitude. He huffed and puffed to himself because he was bored, and he usually looked unhappy. He had once worked at an advertising agency among creative people and so I knew that he must be thinking that he was wasting his life because he was not using any of the creative talent that he had. Margaret sometimes stayed in bed and was reluctant to help Dorothy. Dorothy, the capable and always loyal trained institutional cook, was about 40 years old in 1965. She could look angelic or be in a black mood that caused me to feel anxious in her company but was always a reliable and competent worker. Jack always worked hard, and I noticed that he had deep philosophical discussions with Don sometimes. He always appeared to be bright and cheerful. I for one never felt that I could discuss anything personal bothering me. I was putting so much effort into always thinking positive thoughts that I felt devastated whenever I thought that any member might think that I was not pulling my weight or that I was negative in my attitude. After the first three years I decided to stop being so controlling of my thoughts and I felt a huge weight had been lifted off my shoulders. In UPO there was no strict supervision or control. Some of us probably brainwashed ourselves into an almost total belief that Max was going to succeed in his aims if we supported him. After the first four years had passed, I knew that there was little hope of UPO being able to achieve its aims. I was not aware of any other people becoming members, and I was probably wasting my youth staying but I stayed on in the hope of possible success — the faith had gone, but Max was trying his best and I still had great respect for him. He was a hard worker, mentally and physically, although his back popped a disc sometimes. There were no regular UPO reports to comply with the law, and to ease the members' concerns — and what had happened to our philosophical discussions? Max had shown no sign of helping anyone in a personal way that he had done when he had been a practising psychologist.

Sometimes Max had talked about positive thinking. I can only remember two times that Max specifically talked to us as a group to keep us united and have faith in the aims of UPO, but he shielded us from the financial and legal problems that UPO faced. We all knew that he had a huge responsibility, and we did not want to have any negative attitudes that would interfere with his efforts. I also think that we all considered that Max was an extraordinarily gifted and an almost infallible man, who was a hero fighting against authority for a better society. He always spoke briskly and positively, but it was Adrienne who was an excellent organiser and supervisor and lively company.

The boom years in The Australia Lounge and Gallery

I became emotionally like a zombie when I worked in The Australia Coffee Lounge. There were periods when I worked day and night for months — up to 19 hours a day, seven days a week. I had only to walk out the door after cleaning up after closing and in one minute I was back at the UPO office. I slept in a bunk in a spare room by the office because the flat upstairs had been sublet. I developed a system to get to sleep quickly or I would not be able to cope with working the long hours — I pictured myself on a train going through a tunnel. It worked; I would be asleep quickly. I still use a similar method sometimes because it allows my mind to stop its usual activity and rest. I had listened to a self-hypnosis lesson that Max had recorded on his Mindpower record label in Wellington. I guess that it was also the beginning of my starting to develop a meditation method.

I rarely saw Max or Adrienne during a long period when I was left to manage The Australia. I coped by not thinking about failure, but I thought that my long hours working seemed to be never-ending. I felt trapped in a life of endless dishes and cleaning, but I tried not to be despondent. Max should have known that I was overworked and should let me know what he was planning, and so I was disappointed because I was not relieved. Perhaps I could have started work later in the mornings, but I could not stop the feeling of guilt — what if something went wrong when I was not there? I could be accused of being irresponsible. However, I trusted that Max and Adrienne were also struggling with the problems of UPO, and the other members were putting energy into trying to make UPO a success.

The exact timing of events so long ago are hazy, but in 1967 Adrienne gave birth to a girl. I probably saw the child only about four times, because Max's mother owned a house on the North Shore and Max and Adrienne lived there in a flat at this time. I am not sure when I was suddenly told to return to live on Rakino, but it was probably the end of 1967.

The nightclub, the stripper, and the police

I became depressed as the months passed on Rakino and I performed my usual lawnmowing and other duties and spent most of the time de-nailing the demolition timber from Motuihe Island. I was concerned that what I was doing was a waste of time because I felt as if I was making no difference to the future of UPO. I had no idea whether the aims of UPO were being achieved.

Adrienne sent an undated letter to Dorothy and me, but it was probably written about February 1969, describing Checkers, a nightclub that Max and Jack had been constructing in Symonds Street, a 10-minute walk from The Australia and the UPO office. I felt perplexed — I felt completely out of the information loop.

I was recalled back to the city during the early months of 1969 to manage The Australia again — probably about March. Soon afterwards, someone informed me that Graeme had left Rakino; he had hitched a passage back to Auckland aboard a barge. I presumed that he had left UPO.

New liquor licensing laws had been in force since October 1967. Hotels and bars no longer had to close at 6 pm and the new laws allowed them to stay open until 10 pm. There must have been a dramatic reduction of trade for the few coffee lounges that been open until late at night. The Australia had probably been the first to stay open late in 1964 — sometimes until midnight or 1 am. Most similar businesses now traded during the day only. I had not socialised outside of work because I was always there or sleeping so had no knowledge of what had been happening outside of my limited social world.

People socialising since the law change now had the option of frequenting a bar in the evenings instead of a coffee lounge or a dancehall. I was disappointed to find that The Australia was now in a run-down condition with very few customers and was no longer open evenings or early mornings. A 17-year-old girl assisted me to do what I could to increase the turnover.

I was confused about the reason for building Checkers, the nightclub. What had a nightclub got to do with the stated aims of UPO? Where did the money come from to finance the construction if The Australia was not making any profit? Max must have persuaded someone to provide the finance for the construction. Will that debt be the final crushing blow for UPO? I assumed that Max hoped to use the income from the nightclub to bankroll UPO. Was there still a mortgage on Rakino? I did not know. The financial status of UPO was a mystery to everyone except Max, and perhaps Don, Jack, and Adrienne. I had a feeling that something was about to finish UPO as a charitable society that I could support.

Checkers was a private club. Max's long-time friend Don was the manager — he was at the door wearing a black suit with a bow tie when I went to have a look when it was open one evening. He looked like a movie star at the Oscars. A very glamorous and chatty 23-year-old blonde hostess named Marilyn welcomed me. Recorded music was playing while about 40 members sat at the tables but there were no live bands performing. The club consisted of two floors with two stages and a high-class restaurant — but no chef — and there was a large basement office. There was a lot of plush carpet and large mirrors on several walls. Adrienne's letter had said that a separate band would perform on each stage — rock and roll on one stage and soul on the other — one dancefloor and stage was on the first floor. I had never heard of soul music. John Battersby's Big Band would be the resident band, and Bobby Davis, a recording star, had been performing there recently. For the times this was an extremely classy premises. However, there cannot have been enough members yet for the club to be financially viable to provide a full programme every night, and so the entertainment must have been trimmed back. Waitresses were wearing outfits like Playboy Bunny Girls, but I was more shocked than impressed. I do not know the details, but around this time Max had a nervous breakdown. He also appeared to be drunk the night that I paid a visit, and I could see that his face had become distorted. It was about three weeks later that I saw Max again and there was no sign of any disfigurement. He had once told me that he had had a mental breakdown before he moved to Auckland and it had distorted his face, but he had used his willpower to train his face muscles to restore their usual appearance.

I thought I must have been dreaming when Max arrived at The Australia for lunch with Marilyn and her six-year-old son one day, because they looked like a family on a holiday outing. I wondered if he was joking when he told me not to tell Adrienne. However, Adrienne came in a few days later and I could not lie to her when she asked me if Max had been in with Marilyn. Her response was instant — she was furious. 'That bastard refused to marry me! Marilyn was a stripper before she worked at Checkers!' Adrienne fumed. Max had not been staying with her lately and was supposed to be sleeping in Checkers' office. As she left, she told me not to mention to Max that she had been asking about him. I was shocked and confused. What had gone wrong to cause such a rift between what I had thought was a perfectly matched — and married — couple?

I had been surprised by the change in Max's personality — he had not been his usual emphatic self but had been acting very boyishly. He had a meeting with Don at The Australia a week later, and he asked me if Adrienne had enquired if he had been in with Marilyn. I was caught between a rock and a hard place — I squirmed as I felt loyal to both Adrienne and Max, but I admitted that Adrienne had been asking about his visit with Marilyn and her son. Thoughtful would best describe Max's demeanour; he gave me the impression that he considered Adrienne was the one who had committed some misdeed. I was wondering if he had fully recovered from his recent breakdown. I did not think that Max was making carefully considered decisions.

I had been walking to Checkers every morning because Max had asked me to vacuum the two levels; there was a lot of carpet. It took me almost two hours every day. I chatted to a man who was the manager and husband of the featured Welsh cabaret singer, Ann Sabine. The couple made world news over the next few months because they had disappeared overseas and abandoned their five children in New Zealand. They never returned. Two of their children are probably still living in New Zealand, according to Google. Ann died in Wales in 2015; her husband was found wrapped in plastic outside her flat. He had been killed by a blow to his head 18 years earlier and had been kept inside for most of that time because Ann had been receiving his pension. She had bragged to everyone about having been a successful Australian Shirley Bassey style cabaret singer, and she always spoke in an obviously fake Australian accent. The reality was that she had not been a consistent success as a professional singer.

Max had managed to keep UPO from collapsing several times in the past, but his latest scheme was about to end in disaster.

It may be interesting to know what entertainment was available prior to this period. The choice was between movies, dancehalls, skating rinks, swimming pools, billiard rooms, horse and dog racing, motor sport and a variety of sports. During the 1960s there had been a gradual easing of the liquor licensing laws. I remember seeing a coffee shop for the first time in 1958 or 1959, in Devonport. Before that the local milk bar was the place to buy a sandwich and have a cup of tea, but the coffee bar stayed open until late at night — even until after midnight. It was called The Caballero, and the original owner was a handsome young man from the Caribbean. I wondered if the coffee bar idea would be a success, but I was surprised when I saw that some people were willing to pay for a drink at night and perhaps a toasted sandwich before they went home. It did not take long before the coffee bar was full of people, even at midnight some nights. Soon another late-night coffee bar had been opened that was not in the shopping centre — The Pink Elephant — and the residents became upset with the noisy midnight crowd, often drunk, and loud music from the jukebox. Alcohol could legally be bought at a hotel, but only between the hours of 10 am and 6 pm.

At the beginning of the 1960s some coffee bars had developed into recreational places to relax and enjoy jukebox music, and live music soon began to become common. Some coffee bars had started to allow drinking alcohol 'under the table', and a popular ballroom, The Peter Pan — near the top of Auckland's main street, Queen Street — was commonly known to allow drinking. I was at a function there in my teens when it was announced: 'Please place your alcohol under the table; the police will be here in five minutes.' When the uniformed police arrived, they had stood at the entrance and chatted to the staff for about 10 minutes and then left. I was astonished at the apparent acceptance of the law being ignored at that one venue.

Nightclubs with live bands had quickly developed and become popular, and local musical heroes were becoming more common. It became obvious that the liquor laws were being ignored.

The liquor laws were relaxed gradually. A very few restaurants were granted a liquor licence to sell alcohol to diners only. Legal permission cost money and was beyond the means for most restauranteurs — Max considered this not only unfair but appeared to be corrupt. Were some people in authority being bribed? Why did some people get fined for breaking the licensing laws and others were not? This anomaly appeared to make Max 'hot' — something corrupt was surely going on.

That is probably why Max and Don came up with the idea of how to be legally serving alcohol — not selling — without kow-towing to the police, authorities, or bribing anyone. The way that Checkers avoided the law applying to licensed premises seemed simple. Members had to deliver their own alcohol during the day; a record would be kept of their delivery and they would receive a card that could be clipped. The card was like a receipt, noting what alcohol had been delivered — for example beer or spirits. When they wanted to order, a waitress would deliver the customers their own alcohol, their card would be clipped and there was a service fee to pay every time they were served.

Utopia becomes a faded dream

Disaster was about to strike. Police had unexpectedly turned up at Checkers' office with the appropriate documents to allow them to legally remove the membership records. Adrienne had apparently vigorously protested — how could business continue without knowing who were members? I had arrived at Checkers one morning and I saw the books being carried away. Max was fuming; later he said that his appeals to the police for the books to be returned promptly, so that Checkers could keep trading, were laughed at. The police were certain that the club had broken the law and did not seem to be interested in listening to any protests. Checkers was unable to open because details about membership or what alcohol they owned were not available. About two weeks later, Max knew that time had run out for UPO. Checkers needed to be operating and attracting new members but that was impossible without records. I had been managing the coffee shop about three months when a very humbled Max told me that UPO was in liquidation. I was not aware of any official society meeting that was convened for members to inform them about the liquidation of the society. Max asked me if I would mind taking a wage and staying to manage the coffee lounge until a buyer could be found. I knew that he was no longer my infallible leader. He was speaking to me like an appreciative friend. I was surprised that I felt no sorrow. I felt a sense of finality.

I make a fresh start

Adrienne, after some final bookwork that she said was because of loyalty to UPO, departed for Sydney with her child, now about two years old. Adrienne told me that she had been correcting anyone calling at Checkers who addressed her as Mrs Rickard — she had reverted to Mrs Hargreaves, her name from her earlier legal marriage.

Max was about 43 years old. He and his lover and child left for Sydney about six weeks later. The following month I was looking for a normal paid job because new owners took over the business. The whole block of shops had a limited life anyway because the adjacent Sheraton Hotel was expanding, and the block where The Australia was would soon be demolished.

I immediately got a paid job. I had no idea what skills I had that would qualify me for a job and I had to familiarise myself with managing my own money again. I felt no disappointment, only relieved that now I finally felt free to plan my own future. I was aware that my hope of a family type of community that would care for people and each other was gone. The consistently positive and emphatic Max, who had originally appeared to have no doubt that what he had visualised for society could be achieved, had overreached.

I had been aware for at least three years that there had been no evidence that Max was directing the members towards achieving the stated aims of UPO. It appeared that having money and members to begin any UPO projects had to be the number one priority, but I had never been told officially that originally there had still been a mortgage to be paid on Rakino.

However, I was never privy to UPO's financial status at any time. I am sure that the members who stayed on to try to help had all been hoping that Max's vision would come to pass, but the years had been slipping away. I was eventually quite restless about the lack of information on UPO's financial status, and the lack of knowledge about Max's plans, or lack of a plan. I was probably like most young men; I would have liked to marry but had put it out of consideration. Without a social life and money, I had not wanted to torture myself by even thinking about it. What sort of lifestyle could I have shared with a young prospective wife?

Establishing a life after UPO

After I had saved some money, I left for Sydney. I still had some faith that Max might start some humanitarian project. When I first arrived in Sydney, I boarded with Max and Marilyn. Max appeared to be his usual pre-breakdown self, but he suddenly left Marilyn after three months; I was a witness when he accused her of meeting up with an ex-boyfriend. Marilyn soon teamed up with another woman and they began work as escorts. I could see what they were planning, and I moved out to live independently. Several months later I had to visit Marilyn for a reason that I cannot recall, and she and another woman had two huge American men lounging around her flat. I guessed that they were American army soldiers on leave from the Vietnam War.

Max ran a high-class introduction agency that he had started in the centre of King's Cross, but he soon sold it. He must have then practised as a psychologist in Potts Point nearby and ran a self-improvement course in the evenings. He had mail order sales of his own Mindpower brand cassettes about counselling or meditation. He had sold televisions from home for extra money, and he had an arrangement to sell a car on behalf of a dealer at least once.

Dr Maxwell Rickard in London, with his wife Joan, 1974

About two years later, Max married Joan, a 32-year-old vegetarian — a warm-hearted, practical, and conservative real estate letting agent. I was a guest as well as his 21-year-old son, who gave a speech. Dorothy was at Max's flat twice while I was visiting, but I never saw her again.

Max and Joan moved to Wembley in London during early 1973 and wrote to me in Sydney several times the same year. He had made a friend of the managers of Arcadia House, a healing centre, and had been offered the chance of a permanent position there a few months later. He gave several lectures, ran courses, and had 11 books prepared that he had written. He was preparing to publish the first one himself using a duplicating machine. He attended a large international parapsychology conference, and he wrote to me that he had received offers to speak in America. Financially he was struggling but money was coming in from the sale of his cassettes and from Joan's wages as a secretary for a quilt manufacturer. Max was pleased to have received an apologetic letter from Graeme, and said he intended to reply. While writing these words, I suddenly remembered that I had coincidentally seen Graeme in Sydney the following year, in December 1974. Graeme had become a successful professional astrologer with an office in a bank building in central Sydney. Dorothy had also written to Max; she had a boyfriend and was sorry, but she was not going to keep in touch any more. Max and Joan moved back to Sydney in 1975.

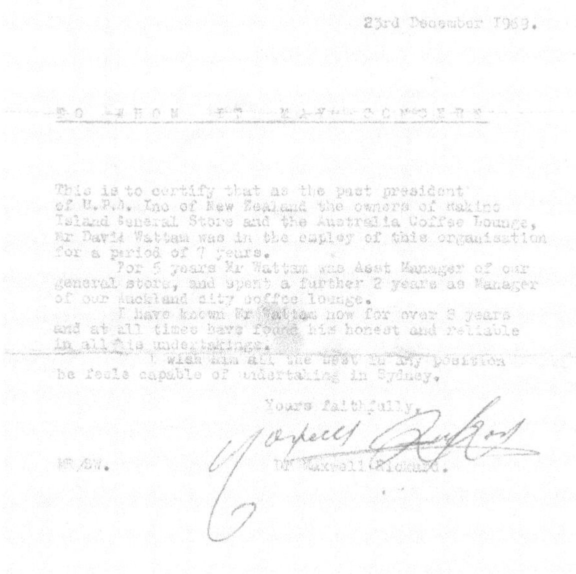

23rd December 1969.

TO WHOM IT MAY CONCERN

This is to certify that as the past president of U.P.A. Inc of New Zealand the owners of Makino Island General Store and the Australia Coffee Lounge, Mr David Wattam was in the employ of this organisation for a period of 7 years.

For 5 years Mr Wattam was Asst Manager of our general store, and spent a further 2 years as Manager of our Auckland city coffee lounge.

I have known Mr Wattam now for over 8 years and at all times have found him honest and reliable in all his undertakings.

I wish him all the best in any position he feels capable of undertaking in Sydney.

Yours faithfully,

Dr Maxwell Rickard.

MR/SW.

Dr Rickard provided the author with this reference

In 1983, when I was living in Auckland again with my Australian partner and our son, they wrote and told me that they were selling their house and then they would move to live in Wellington, where Max's mother lived. Max's mother had informed him that she was leaving the house in Glenfield, where they had once been living in Auckland, to him in her will.

It was probably during 1978 that Rosemary, Adrienne's sister, made headline news in the *8 O'clock* — a Saturday sports newspaper. It announced that she had died after following an unqualified doctor Milan Brych's treatment for cancer. She had been hoping to survive to see Christmas with her family. I had visited her and her husband while I was on a holiday from Australia. She had become a qualified district nurse. She had told me that she was enthusiastic about being treated for cancer by a revolutionary method. Unfortunately, her treatment was ineffective, and most of her doctor's patients were reported to have died. Now so had Rosemary.

The article claimed that Rosemary had suffered from neglect while she had lived on Rakino Island, although I understood that after the first three years living on Rakino she had moved to board with a family in Auckland to complete her education. She had always looked cheerful when I was living there, but Adrienne had treated her sternly and I could never understand why. I had presumed that Max would have intervened if Adrienne had been unreasonable with her discipline. Rosemary had two children when I visited her. I was puzzled when her husband angrily grumbled that adults should have intervened to protect her.

Milan Brych was disbarred by the New Zealand Medical Council in 1974. He relocated to the Cook Islands, where more deaths from his bogus treatment followed, and then he moved on to Queensland, and then to California, where he was eventually given a jail sentence, according to Google. He was released in 1986.

In 1987, I was surprised when Max and Joan contacted me, and we meet up the next day. Both looked very thoughtful — Joan had been diagnosed with cancer. I had assumed that she would be receiving treatment and had at least several years still to live.

The crumpled hero

Within 12 months Max showed up again behaving irrationally at the restaurant that I owned with a business partner in Auckland City. His voice almost broke as he told me that Joan had died, and it had been soul destroying to see her suffer. His manner towards me had changed; he talked to me like an old friend that he could confide in but was drinking heavily and unable to focus. Suddenly he blurted out that he had had sex with Margaret all those years ago. 'What am I to do if she grabs my hand as I walk past?' he said. I was surprised at the immature excuse, but I was not shocked. His admission must have confirmed what I instinctively knew. Max was admitting that he had been dishonest when he had inferred that he had not had sex with Margaret. He had belittled her and punched her to cover up his own weakness. Now I questioned my own attitude; why had I forgotten the incident so quickly? Even if his striking Margaret was explained away in my mind as frustration being expressed in response to a loathsome lie that she had told, I should have taken the view that it was still an assault. At that time, I had had so much respect for Max that it amounted to awe, and I never questioned any of Max's decisions. My memory of the incident had soon receded into the past.

During a discussion in a café, Max started talking quietly to me and his eyes darted around — he thought that people nearby might be spying on us. He was trying to organise support to stop the proposed demolition of a block of shops in Karangahape Road and wanted to open a hamburger shop in the block. At his motel he told me he had had goods transported by a taxi truck company and some furniture had been damaged. He showed me a small table as an example and deliberately damaged it more by pulling on a leg. He told me he was having a serious dispute with the taxi company managers. He appeared to be thoughtful, but he was obviously unhinged. What had happened to the Max that had been fighting for truth and honesty? He did not seem to be aware that he was behaving like a con man. He was speaking to me as if I were a confidant who sympathised with him.

Three months later he visited again and was completely sober and rational but was still not his old self. He left for Wellington after a few days.

Another month later, I was bewildered when he turned up again to stay with me driving a 16-year-old Rolls-Royce and accompanied by a partying 20-year-old young woman and behaving like an irresponsible youth. He told me jokingly that the government — his pension — was paying for the car. When they departed about six days later, he handed me a signed IOU for $2,200 that he said he owed me up to that point. I had seen little of the couple because I had to go to work.

More time passed; dates are hazy, but I am trying to get close to the facts, but these visits after Joan died all happened over about 12 months.

Max turned up again sober with a pet Scottish terrier and stayed overnight. He was not drinking any more. He was very subdued and appeared to be prematurely senile. He was befuddled although he was only 62 years old. It became obvious that since his wife had died the pressure of trying to achieve his goals without her support and grounding had become too much and he had cracked. He had no pride left. Perhaps I was the only person that he thought could understand him and knew about the lofty goals that he had failed to achieve. I remember that on one of his last visits he had showed me a clipping from a magazine that was advertising liquid peroxide and explained its uses. He said that he was using the advertisement to give him ideas for his own promotion about a simple cancer cure. He spoke in a very vague way as if he did not really know what he was talking about. About two months later, a downtrodden-looking Max, who said that he had been in Wellington, called to see me at the restaurant. I had a business partner who understood that in the past I had had a reverence for Max, so she was very understanding when Max appeared to be acting erratically sometimes. He asked me if I had seen a current affairs programme on television interviewing people mentioning him by name, who were complaining that Max was trying to raise money for a bogus cancer treatment. I told him that I had seen the programme on my night off. Max spoke very quietly on this visit — he was no longer the confident leader that I had known. He acted like a beaten man whose dreams had been crushed and who had no pride left. I wondered if he would ever recover from his latest mental setback, and had he done anything illegal?

I do not know what became of him; I never saw him again. If he were still alive, he would be 94 years old. I still possess the letters from him and Joan from London in 1973, and one from Sydney in 1983. They provided me with the information I have included in this story.

Max should have had the professional knowledge to be aware of what had happened to cause his breakdown. He had obviously been delusional on some of his visits.

I coincidentally picked up a *Metro* magazine from 1988 that I found lying around. A featured article about the Auckland gulf islands reported that Max had been trying to rustle up support to stand for a seat on the Waiheke Island Council, but he was being treated as a joke, according to the feature writer. On one of his visits to see me during 1988, he was sober but did not appear to be his old self. He told me that when Rakino had been surveyed the wharf area had purposely been left off a survey map; this apparently had some relevance to his visit to Waiheke. Rakino had been placed under the jurisdiction of the Auckland City Council since the UPO days; the Waiheke Local Board now had authority over Rakino Island. On one visit Max had requested that I drive him to see a prominent barrister, but his meeting had been very brief. I got the impression from a very subdued and frustrated-looking Max that he could not convince the barrister to help him with his problem — whatever that was. On that day Max did not appear to be mentally competent.

On his visits to see me he was talking to me as if I were one of his confidants. In previous years he had been a self-confident imperious leader but was often a big brother who appeared to not want to worry his members with UPO's management problems.

Max had once commented that powerful men could not be constrained by one woman. He did not want any woman telling him what to do and he resented any restrictions by authorities that he considered were unreasonable. For example, he had furious arguments with the person who wrote the infringement notices for having a coffee lounge sandwich board on the footpath, breaking council by-laws. Why were dozens of other sandwich boards on the footpath not getting fined? He often thought that he was being singled out by authorities. He was not afraid to confront anyone about perceived injustices. In 1964 a policeman had asked me if The Australia was owned by the strange owner of Rakino Island he had heard about. I told Max, and that led to an investigating senior officer having a long meeting with us both. Max thought that rumours about him could be circulating among the Auckland police.

I left Auckland in 1997 and moved 135 kilometres south to live in Hamilton. About two years later, I saw two women ahead of me in a crowd. I was amazed to see that one of them was Margaret. She confirmed what she had said all those years ago and added that Max had had sex with her several other times. She surprised me by telling me that she had supported Max because she had regarded him as her guru! When she left UPO she had met and married her future husband and had two children. The elegant woman with her was her 23-year-old daughter. I met her 17-year-old son at her home another day.

Her older husband had died several years before, and Margaret had been practical enough to work to pay the balance of the mortgage on her house. About 1999 she appeared being interviewed on a television programme investigating whether electric shock treatment should be permitted as part of the mental health system. She had told me that for her the so-called treatment had been terrifying. 'How can human beings do that to another human being?' she asked. She was a member of a Hamilton patients' rights advocacy organisation.

I had a firm belief that I had not completely wasted my time when I was a member of UPO. I was still confident that there is a universal truth and justice, and every thought and action are automatically registered. As you read about what transpired for me in the years following my UPO period you may come to believe that I have proved to myself, through incredible personal experiences, that there is an all-inclusive natural law that regulates everything. Now that I have had more experience about legal matters, I know that a charitable society is legally required to have a register of members, and there should be regular meetings and reports. The members should vote for the officers who represent them. There was only one meeting of UPO that appeared to be official — the first one; after that Max, assisted by regular consultations with lawyers and accountants, must have become a one-man band. As I write this memoir I still wonder — was I ever a registered member? Should I have ever had a vote?

After the collapse of UPO I wanted to continue to live a life that I would never regret in my old age. During the seven years in UPO I had trained myself to work diligently until the work that I was assigned was completed to a good standard, even when exhausted.

After the failure of the society and a few years of financial struggle, I eventually inched towards owning my own business. My plan was to concentrate on being successful financially so that I would be able to follow my vague dream of developing mental clarity and an inner wisdom to 'help people'. How I was going to achieve that objective I did not know. Within four years of leaving the society I had a partner who was often severely mentally ill. We had one child and I had to focus and try to become financially secure. Ten years later my partner and I parted amicably, but we remain in regular contact.

Chapter 2
The ideals of my youth resurface

IN 1995, I SUDDENLY DECIDED TO IMMEDIATELY reassess where I was with my life. I was 54 years old and aware that I had not achieved the deepest desire of my youth — to live a harmonious life through a greater understanding of myself and other people, and to make a worthwhile contribution to society. I recognised that I was restless and depressed, and I needed to have some interests that satisfied me as I prepared myself for my eventual retirement. It seemed to be almost too late at this stage of my life for this dream to come true. I was aware that my ambitions to seek spiritual fulfilment had always been in the background.

I recalled that when I was 26 years old, in 1967, I had been intrigued when a young woman customer spread out some ordinary playing cards on a table in The Australia coffee lounge that I was managing and predicted that I would have two girlfriends within three weeks, and that I would eventually receive a legacy. I was working every day and night in the coffee lounge and any time off seemed impossible, so I was surprised when an opportunity came to have some time off. When a part-time employee, a student, offered to take responsibility for the business for two nights. I shyly asked a young woman for a date but did not get a positive response and so I asked another woman, and she accepted. The first woman returned, and she also agreed to date me. Unintentionally, I did have two temporary girlfriends, but as I had not been having any social life for five years, I had no idea where to go or how to get there. The dating could not have led to any future relationship because I did not have any personal money saved and so was unable to plan for my future.

Twenty-five years passed before another woman laid out some cards and made some predictions for me which came true, but she had used tarot cards. I had never seen them before. This woman repeated the prediction that I had been given in 1967 — I had a legacy coming. I did eventually receive an unexpected inheritance 34 years after the first prediction — in 2001.

Here I was in 1995, thinking that card reading could possibly be my retirement interest; if I could learn how to read cards, then I would have an extra social skill and maybe help people at the same time. I had been interested in mysteries since childhood; I had observed an old relative who was visiting my grandparents when I was about 10 years old — she had given a reading while she peered at the dregs of the tea leaves inside a cup. I felt certain that there was some mysterious truth that could be discovered. I had tried water divining with the forked branch of a willow tree at about this time but did not feel any response. In 1958, I volunteered to be a subject for a well-known Australian touring hypnotist Franquin, when hypnotism shows were popular. I went on to the stage with about 10 other volunteers, but I did not succumb to his suggestion to sleep on the count of three like most of the other volunteers.

It is true that it is never too late to try something new; my life was about to change dramatically.

I located the second card reader again, although two years had passed since I had seen her. She told me that she had been trained to read tarot cards and studied numerology at a parapsychology school.

Chapter 3
Parapsychology school
Counselling with tarot cards and numerology

To my surprise, I located the North Shore Parapsychology School from the phone book. It was in Milford, on Auckland's North Shore. I became a student at an evening course once a week for three months and was astounded with what I was being taught.

I had felt apprehensive as I joined the pupils in my large class. They were in the 20–55-year age range and appeared to be conservative, intelligent, and very attentive. All except three were women. I think that I was expecting budding fortune tellers but that would be foolishly unrealistic.

'Your lives are never going to be the same again,' said the elderly grey-haired school principal on the first night. Her name was Francie Williams. She dressed simply and appeared to be a very ordinary person but was soon to demonstrate that she was not at all ordinary. Her face bore faint signs of having had a stroke in the past. She was patient but was quick to firmly correct any misunderstanding about her teachings.

Francie recommended that we buy the Rider pack of tarot cards and advised us to use her method at first until we gain experience. This system was not hocus-pocus, but a genuine practice that could help people. I soon found to my amazement that the cards indicated what conditions were present in a person's life, and predictions were also possible. We used a classmate's birthday in tarot card-reading demonstrations to provide additional numerological information, such as probable personality traits, and were warned not to check up other people's personal lives unless they gave permission. Dress in a business-like manner if we were to have clients, not like a fortune teller in a Hollywood movie. 'Be professional, because soon these methods will be an acceptable way to counsel people,' said Francie. We were shown how to give a personal reading or an impersonal business reading. Everything was revealed: finances, relationships, family, travel, and health. I made certain to attend every class. By the end of the tarot reading course three months later we were shown how we could give a 'medical' reading that revealed medical conditions such as heart problems. It occurred to me that I could use the cards to do a medical reading for a car, or a house, and pets. I surprised some people when I read for them and told them about problems looming for their car, or registration fees or overdue fines. The water poured into a friend's house from a leaky roof that I had warned him about just after he had bought it.

Francie had high principles. She advised us to ask permission from a higher source before we started to read for anyone, or to at least have a positive attitude. An example Francie gave was a prayer. She recommended that sitting quietly alone before a reading would help to settle the mind to be more receptive to intuition. I wondered if this was a type of meditation. What was meditation anyway? I did not really know yet.

The teacher has a spirit friend

A few weeks later Francie told us that often during her life she had heard a friendly voice that she had named Fred. She casually told us that this parapsychology school was supported by the White Brotherhood, teachers of wisdom, a fraternity of evolved people who had lived on earth but were now in spirit. None of my classmates appeared to be fazed when they heard this. I thought it would be fantastic if I had a friendly voice giving me encouragement.

Lately I had been feeling like a lost soul, wondering where my life was heading, but now I felt a surge of excitement. When I read the cards, I was seeing evidence that there must be a natural spiritual system always present.

Francie told our class that many years before she had been given some tarot cards but could not understand the instructions that came with them, so she put the card pack aside. One day she saw the cards glowing and she heard a voice saying: 'Pick up the cards. We will teach you.' I had always wanted to believe that I might take a different road one day and meet a truly wise person who might have a very ordinary appearance, just like a character in a fairy tale. Was Francie such a person?

Francie told her class that because some people were naturally psychic, they might prefer to change to a method of their own later — because they knew intuitively what the cards were indicating. Francie did not tell us to refer to the instruction manual that was in the card pack; we had a folder of her dictated notes about her own method and examples that had been typed out.

Francie and Dean Collier, another teacher at the parapsychology school who taught some of the classes that I attended, taught that any good that comes through them was received from a higher source and it was detrimental to their own spiritual progress to accept personal praise because pride retards spiritual growth.

In the numerology class, students were told that everything in the universe is vibrating, and numbers represent a rate of vibration. The numbers that represent our birthday are indicating our inner potential — our character. We were born when we were because that was what we deserved, and we have free will to develop to our full potential. We are not being punished by a higher power; we are given an opportunity to have worthwhile experiences to keep evolving. We should develop our intuition, the voice of our conscience. This is 'the still small voice' mentioned in Psalms, according to Francie.

I decided to take an additional course on 'spiritual numerology' taught by Dean; I wanted to understand myself better and perhaps be uplifted by hearing about what may be possible for me to discover within myself. Because it was clear now that there was a pattern to life, I wanted to take detailed notes of every comment of Dean's, so I scribbled hurriedly during his lessons.

'You have just completed a spiritual cycle,' said Dean. 'You are starting a new cycle.' Cycles go from one to nine, which may be a completion before moving on to a new cycle of life — 10, 11, etc. — or the cycle may be repeated starting at number one again, going through similar experiences all over again. The aim should be to keep progressing spiritually to promote soul growth. Dean told me that I had latent spiritual or magnetic healing gifts, as well as clairvoyant capabilities, and I would always be safe from financial disaster. I was capable and adaptable and was a person who could get on with everyone but needed freedom of movement. 'That explains why you ask me so many questions!' said Dean. I certainly did.

Being told I had untapped qualities soothed any concerns about not being worthy to be in these classes. Over the following years I was astounded when I gradually began to 'unfold' some of these qualities. To this day I have all the notes.

Pendulums

Francie told us that it was possible to use a pendulum to locate physical problems in a human or animal body. Using a pendulum can also be used to locate water, or water pipes underground — in fact, anything sought after can usually be located. This system is called 'dowsing'. A specific question must be clearly asked before commencing. Maybe it would be decided that a left swing of the pendulum would be a 'no' response and a right swing is a 'yes'. These days I use it to answer any question that I want to know the answer to, such as: 'Are my lost car keys in the lounge?' Sometimes I want to know if it is going to rain that day.

I had observed Francie's husband Rex using this method to locate problems areas on a patient. I was told he did not have to use the pendulum — his hands passing close to a client's body could locate any problem areas, and he had clients for healing massages. Thirty years previously a man had shown me that if he held a pendulum over food it would swing with a 'no' answer over food that had poor nutritional qualities, such as white sugar.

Tarot cards — 'You're pregnant!'

At home I practised with the tarot cards for several hours a week. When I laid the cards out after shuffling, I was not always confident that there was any obvious meaning triggered in my mind. When a young woman asked me to practise by doing a reading for her, I shuffled the cards clumsily because I had never been a card player, then I laid the cards out as taught.

'Ask the client if they want the straight truth,' Francie had advised her class. The young woman told me to be straight with her.

'It seems as if you're pregnant,' I said with as much confidence as I could muster.

'I'm not pregnant!' the blushing woman said as she stamped off. 'I haven't even got a boyfriend!'

The next day she met me and spoke quietly to me.

'You worried me, so I went to the pharmacy for a pregnancy test kit. I *am* pregnant!' 'How can you get pregnant if you haven't got a boyfriend?' I asked. The woman looked embarrassed and frustrated. She had one date with a man and had sex. He was a doctor, but his rooms were not up to a professional standard, so she had not wanted to continue to have a relationship with him. I was stimulated to practise with my cards much more often — and believe what they indicated.

I see auras and start a diary

I started to record briefly in a diary what significant dreams and psychic events I experienced. I wanted to be able to look back for encouragement as time passed if I became discouraged that I was not making progress towards improved spiritual understanding.

'Spiritual' was not a word that I would use for these teachings at this stage of my learning. It took several years to become aware that there were two descriptive terms that were used to help to explain the experiences that I observed: spiritual and psychic. Reading about something is not striving and achieving a result unless it is put into practice, and spiritual included being ethical. I did not know at this stage that spiritual states surpassed psychic dimensions. Was it possible to have a personal experience that verified book knowledge? That interest became my focus. There must be a source: the frequencies, vibrations, or dimension that Francie called the 'akasha' — where she said that everything that ever happens or is thought about is recorded — must be the source. Books written in English sometimes contained the words 'the astral light' and 'etheric' that had a similar meaning. Over the following years I became convinced that some explanations are the accumulated knowledge of thousands of years of sages' meditations. It needs to be understood that attempts to explain what is invisible to most people have been made in many languages and cultures. Translations should make sense in a philosophical sense but may not, although they are accurate from the grammarian's or philologist's point of view.

During one class Francie told the class that the cheerful laughter heard coming from the next classroom was from a young girls' aura class. As she spoke, I was startled to see a pale glow around her head. 'Excuse me, Francie!' I called out jubilantly: 'When you said "aura", I saw a colour appear around your head.'

'What colour did you see?' asked Francie, unfazed.

'A light greenish yellow,' I responded.

'That's okay,' said Francie, and she continued with her teaching.

Francie casually remarked that it would be interesting for us to learn about auras. A personal aura is the result of the field of force that is in and around everybody and has been described as a vibrating electromagnetic energy field. There are many of these fields in the human body and some are of major importance. The vibrations generate colours that can be seen naturally by some people.

When I directed my thoughts to think more about the unseen side of life, energy, or psychic centres or as some say 'sacred' centres within my own body, must have gradually become more active. As the people in the East have known for ages past, these centres are like spinning wheels of energy throughout the body; they call them chakras. In many people they are not operating as well as they should — they are like a dim candle barely noticeable in the dark. If a life of high ideals is contemplated and consistently thought about and attempts made to make the ideal a reality, the wheels become more energised, and they spin faster. Each centre emits the colour of its own distinct energy produced by its individual vibration. I was seeing the result of my recent efforts to put the school's teachings into practice.

Aura photographs

The operator of a computerised camera that produced photographs that revealed personal auras was at the school one evening. I had a sitting with him. When I saw the result, I felt a thrill when I saw that there were four large orange balls of light evenly spaced outside my body. The other students' pictures were obviously different. I was later to learn we were at different stages of spiritual development and would each have our own latent qualities that would need to be unfolded before they could be indicated in an aura photograph.

I had another picture taken some months later using the same camera and was extremely excited when the resulting image showed that the main colour had changed from orange: there was now a large arc of white around my head and shoulders with a trace of yellow around the outer edge. I was certain by now that the colours in an aura photograph were an indication of the inner intentions and level of psychic awakening of the subject. I was thrilled, because the photo seemed to verify that there must be a spiritual path — it was not just New Age wishful thinking! For the next couple of years, the colours that soon became predominant in my photographs were blue, green, violet, and indigo,

The colours emanating from each of the energy centres is obviously different. Starting at the base of the spine and finishing at the crown of the head, the colours are red, orange, yellow, green, blue, indigo, and violet or white on the crown — white is the combination of all the colours. The predominant colours must be from the chakras that were now vibrating faster. A Google search will confirm these colours as aura colours. They emanate from each organ of the body.

About 12 months later I had another aura photograph taken. I was certain that the obvious recent colour changes in the photographs of me indicated that I had altered psychically or spiritually in a significant way and I was no longer feeling depressed. I wanted to continue to unfold my true nature. I started to spend much less time watching TV and avoided violent programmes, preferring to watch documentaries or study Francie and Dean's parapsychology lessons. If I occupied my mind with thoughts of self-improvement, I was certain that I would have more mental clarity.

Time seemed precious to me now because I was 56 years old, and the feeling of sadness caused by a lack of progress towards the goals of my younger years had dissipated.

Spiritual highlighting

Cynthia, an elegantly dressed young woman from one of my parapsychology classes, had asked me if I would do a private tarot card reading for her. I was reading to her at home from notes related to our discussion.

'Cynthia,' I said, 'some sentences are highlighted with a violet colour.' That had seemed so impossible that I did not know whether I should have said anything. How could this be happening?

Cynthia responded matter-of-factly: 'There are two orange balls hovering above your head.' I tried looking away to the side for a few seconds, thinking that the highlighting may have been caused by an optical effect, but the violet colour remained. After a short time, the violet colour disappeared. Over the next 25 years psychic or spiritual experiences gradually became commonplace.

One evening, instead of having the usual lesson at school, some students from classes that were being taught other subjects at the school volunteered to have our class do a tarot reading for them. One young woman surprised me. She told me, 'There Is a man in spirit standing behind you,' she said. 'He is wearing a black suit and a top hat and carries a cane; he will help you with your readings. I was brought up in a place named Spirit Bay, and I do see people "in spirit",' she said.

Francie had mentioned that when she looked out over her class, she would see many people from the spirit world sitting in the chairs or standing around listening to the teachings. 'They're catching up on what they didn't learn when they were still in a body,' she explained. 'They continue to learn in the spirit world — unless they don't want to.' I felt a sense of relief that I had found teachers that could demonstrate what they were talking about.

My ability to keep an open mind comforted me because at last I was truly mentally free and seemed to be relieved of a mental burden.

Spiritual study books

I noticed a second-hand bookshop in a run-down suburb as I drove past. On a whim — or using my inner tuition — I parked my car and went in. A clairvoyant woman had told me that I would be good at astrology.

'Some astrology books were brought in this morning. Over there,' the man said, indicating a dilapidated cardboard box. 'But I've sold some already. You can have anything that's left in there for ten dollars.'

Books that I would be browsing over in the next few years were in the box. Someone had been doing the same types of study that I was now doing, but about 30 years or more before. Someone had been attending courses at the Theosophical Society, whose billboard I had often seen. The society promotes universal brotherhood and has a library available where anyone can study religions and philosophies of the world. There was a book in the box written by Doctor Paul Brunton, *The Secret Path*. He wrote about his travels in India in the early twentieth century, looking for what remained of genuine spirituality. He was attempting to explain to Westerners there was a secret path that was a pathway to spiritual understanding: meditation. Another book was *The Training and Work of an Initiate* by Dion Fortune, who explained that spiritual progress was like climbing a mountain: after you have struggled to climb the spiritual mountain and eventually found your own spiritual path, you will arrive at a certain point where you will be met by your master, who will encourage you to continue the rest of your climb. I was now certain I was being guided to find useful answers to my lifelong spiritual questions after all my years of searching and hoping.

But had a master already chosen me?

By now I was positive that I was receiving some spiritual assistance from 'somewhere'. It seemed as if I was often being guided in the right direction to assist my progress towards what I had always desired: understanding myself and my role in the world.

I began to be open about what I was learning when I spoke to friends and acquaintances. Unfortunately, I am certain that most of them were not aware of any other dimensions and were not interested in discussing the possibility.

I practise seeing auras

Practising seeing auras is a good way to rest your mind from random thoughts. It was possible to see my own aura by looking in the mirror at any point on my face or body for about 15 seconds, then moving my gaze about 10 centimetres to one side. There might be green around an ear, for example, but several layers of differing shades of green. This method requires calming and focusing your mind. There needs to be a strong artificial light or plenty of light in the room from the sun. The emotional state and mental quality of our consciousness is registered in our aura. A clairvoyant can get a good indication of another person's *present* state of mind — including mental, spiritual, and emotional states — by the colours that are automatically registered in their aura. As well as the main energy centres, there are many other centres — there is an integrated system through which all the forces to maintain life are always circulating.

Some sensitive people feel another person's pain from an injury or illness in a corresponding part of their own body. One clairvoyant I met could tell what operations a person had undergone in the past because she could see the result in that person's body. Individual chakras are known to be associated with organs of the body.

Colour psychology

The second year that I attended the parapsychology school I enrolled in Dean Collier's class on Colour Psychology — a unique counselling system devised by Francie. I repeated the course later under Francie's tuition. Each student did a coloured sketch in response to a subject suggested by the tutor, such as My Family Life or My Experience at School.

These sketches gave an indication of the inner emotions and circumstances of the person being counselled. The drawing could be just a simple basic sketch — a detailed artistic drawing was not required. The underlying emotional condition of the person who was requesting counselling would be revealed because of certain colour arrangements and other factors in the drawings. Because of the depth of personal information revealed, the small class was sworn to never reveal the method to anyone who was not suitably qualified.

The person being counselled was asked to write their name and birth date on a blank sheet of paper. There will be indications in the drawing of the background to their present situation, and they must be guided carefully to understand that *they* have provided the drawing that lays out how their past has affected the present. They needed to be encouraged to be honest with themselves and face up to the past situations that may still be affecting the present. The students practised on each other. I knew now that being very academic must have little to do with the ability to apply spiritual or psychic knowledge.

We had been taught to make a *visual* selection from an assortment of coloured pencils; I decided that I would draw a sketch representing my childhood years using coloured pencils chosen *randomly* to see what the result would be. I headed up a blank page: My Family. I named each family member and blindly grasped a coloured pencil to represent them and then sketched them as a tree. I continued doing that until all my family was represented as trees. The trees' positions on the page and the colours I used indicated my own psychological impression of each member of my family correctly.

I was certain that the spiritual teachers of history were attempting to tell their listeners about the presence of this faculty, this inherent ability. Information is always immediately available to receptive enquirers. My previous belief in a cosmic justice was well founded — a recording angel was mentioned in the Christian Bible, and karma and 'as you sow, you reap' were ancient attempts to explain the concept; a Personal God need not be blamed — or praised.

A patient's experiences that may cause them problems could be recognised in their colour drawings, and a patient would have the opportunity to recall the memory and to realise that they need to face up to the truth about themselves. The teachers explained that disharmony can cause serious problems in the soul, so the client had to be encouraged to understand the necessity of forgiving themselves for their own perceived past sins — growth processes — as well as forgiving any people that may have wronged the client. These memories that are locked away do not want to be unlocked by the patient, but if they are unlocked the patient can face it and clear it and spiritual and physical health should follow.

This method, developed by Francie, is quite different to other systems that are in more common use in recent times. The patient has an opportunity to understand the circumstances that shaped their life.

Spirit possession

Francie had a surprise for the class near the end of the colour psychology course. She told us that we should be aware that there can be spirit possession, but not as extreme as depicted in the movies.

'I am going to play a cassette tape for you,' she told us. 'I don't let random people listen to this. I want you to be aware of what can happen to some people. You may get a case like this, but it is rare. A woman would start speaking in a man's voice whenever her husband attempted to make love to her. Her husband thought that because he had some spiritual knowledge, he could handle the situation, but one day he decided that he was not coping, so he telephoned me for assistance and decided to record what happened.'

Francie told the class that some people listening could get very alarmed.

We heard a man's voice talking very slowly. The words were distorted but the voice was chilling — a rasping, threatening, loud whisper. Francie was heard arriving and immediately she could be heard commanding the spirit to leave: 'In the name of Christ!' This must have achieved what was necessary because

Francie told the class that the couple's relationship returned to normal.

'The intruding spirit was her father,' Francie told us. 'He was jealous of the woman's husband and wanted her to love only him, even though he was "dead". Do not worry unduly,' said Francie, 'because if all of us always take the precaution of asking for protection, we would be safe. The spirit of the father was in a very confused state. Spirit beings are not always aware that they are no longer in a physical state. When I was a child, I woke up one night and was terrified when I saw my "dead" parents looking youthful and very much alive standing at the foot of my bed.

Over the following years I was to learn from teachers — and Google — who said that some spirits want to linger in the earth's atmosphere after their physical death. They are called pisachas in some Asian countries — ghosts. They may try to cling to a live body so that they can continue enjoying earthly experiences. When they had their own physical body, they died prematurely because of their risky activities, but they cannot move on spiritually until their allotted time on earth is due.

Me, New Age?

For about 10 years, I had aura pictures taken regularly and when I looked at them and could see that I appeared to have evidence that I had grown psychically or spiritually, I felt comforted. Sometimes some physical proof such as an aura photograph can be consoling when spiritual progress appears to have slackened. The photographs were much clearer and detailed than what I could see with my own vision. The camera operator told me many years later that the original camera had malfunctioned and could not be repaired. When he sought in the USA for a replacement, he carefully read the printed material that explained their capabilities. Some of them were only able to produce a picture of colours selected *randomly* by the inbuilt computer. The operator could tell which equipment was producing a photograph of colours that he could verify could be seen clairvoyantly.

Sometimes I would find it amusing when I saw a person walking down the street with their aura flowing along with them as if trying to stay attached to their body. When the water in a washbasin was apparently a violet colour or green or blue, the colour was emanating from my hands while I washed them and showed up easily against the whiteness of the hand basin. If I rested my hand on a white wall and then removed it, a fading coloured handprint remained.

I carried my tarot cards everywhere for the following four years or so because I felt empowered because of my newly acquired knowledge. The instruction that I had received at the parapsychology school was an invisible key that had opened a spiritual-psychic door.

I was bursting to teach everyone what I had learned — that there is more to life than the material world around us, but I have a natural shyness and struggled to give a public talk at this time. Perhaps some people would think that I am talking nonsense, but if the methods I am using are working and by applying them I extend my mind's comprehension, then I should share any knowledge that I have and bear the antagonism and misunderstandings of some people. My persistent search for truth was being rewarded by results and I felt exhilarated.

I was soon surprised to find that there were often opportunities for meeting people with similar interests. I had not noticed that many modern attitudes and interests were called 'New Age', such as channelling, auras, energies, crystals, spiritual healing, herbal remedies, Bach flowers, reflexology, reiki, and various massage techniques. It was now 1997.

Chapter 4
Praying for answers

A lucid dream

Is it possible for an ordinary person to glean genuine knowledge about spiritual matters? I could research the writings of the scholars of each religion, but that probably would take several lifetimes — and I am not a scholar. If I did attempt to sort the wheat from the chaff, how would I know what was chaff? But why should I have to read anything to be in touch with a spiritual dimension? I believed that it should not be necessary to go looking for a spiritual state that was probably already present. Surely *every* generation should have its spiritual teachers and exemplars. Spiritual assistance and knowledge must have been available *prior* to scriptures being compiled, and prior to symbols representing speech being invented. The ancient Sanskrit word 'buddh' is a word that I recently found out means to awaken to the reality of a divine life: to know, and to recognise that we have a transcendental self.

Knowledge which is 'heard' is called Shruthi in India — or the Word of God by Christians — cosmic words of wisdom received wholly from a divine source by seers or rishis in ancient times; but why only in ancient times? Would those people receiving Shruthi in modern times, perhaps while meditating, be ignored if they spoke out? Do scriptures have to be ancient to be acceptable? Are the established religions closed to acknowledging additional information, or clarification of previous Shruthi, from an apparently divine source? Surely the heavens have not disappeared. Theologians consider that their efforts to unravel the mysteries signified by ancient writings assist the faithful to understand and clarify teachings of the past; but did the various religions eventually become too materialistic? Did they become organisations that have a focus on *control* of the followers of the religion? Do religious leaders compel their followers to believe their interpretations of scriptures without *testing* the truth of them?

I began a regular habit of attempting to not only acknowledge but also feel that I had a genuine connection to a divine source. About 20 years previously I had started to become aware that when I was caught up in extremely stressful circumstances, somehow there eventually arose opportunities to find a way forward if I was patient and did my best to be positive. I would list all the possible options and then I would arrive at a conclusion that felt right, but I had never considered that a prayer could alter the natural law of cause and effect. However, if anyone feels that they should pray, then the prayer or invocation must be heartfelt and from a person who is willing to give service to humanity — there must be an intense yearning. This attitude should clean the windows of the intuition. These aspirations may be perceived in an individual's aura by a suitably perceptive person.

There were unanswered questions about the source of the information that was revealed by laying out tarot cards. The akasha was the terminology that the parapsychology teachers had called the source, and they had talked about higher vibrations, spheres, and levels of consciousness. This spiritual atmosphere, I eventually discovered, had various levels. Consider that in the not-too-distant past when hearing radio waves was not possible, it became possible because inventors discovered a system to decipher the vibrations and make them audible to the human ear by distinguishing one frequency from another. Radar can see in the dark, and microwaves and X-rays are not visible. The telephone had seemed a miraculous tool when first invented; Native Americans in the United States called the telegraph talking wires. When I was about nine years old, I could hear faint music that I received via a crystal set, a primitive apparatus that allowed me to hear radio signals transmitted from radio stations, even from overseas, using a crystal as the detector. Many rays and vibrations are in force simultaneously, but some people can separate psychic frequencies from the mix of currents flowing around them, and some people can automatically discern the purely spiritual messages.

By now there had been ample evidence provided to me that there was a spiritual plan. Somehow faculties within me that I had not known existed had started to function, or function more successfully. I was now certain that it was possible to advance psychically and spiritually if the intellect of the mind was modified by the intuition. Francie and Dean had indicated that love for all humanity was a condition to which everyone must eventually evolve.

Every morning when I woke up, I tried to remember this thought: 'Do I really need to read and study endlessly to find the truth that I am yearning for?' This was really a plea — I did not want a lot of opinions and philosophies. My concept of God at this time was of a supreme Intelligence that was unknowable in a human way but had control over the universe, so that it functioned in a balanced way through natural laws. Surely there must be provision for love, justice, and truth to operate. My plea was really expressing a desire in thought form that should be registering in the akasha and have a result.

A few weeks later, I suddenly found myself awake from a deep dreamless sleep to find myself floating. When I looked around there was nothing tangible to be seen, only dim light everywhere like an overcast day. It was an incredibly serene experience. There was complete silence and peace. My vision was clear; I was able to think and decide where to look. When I recovered from my surprise, I knew that something spectacular had happened and I quickly focused mentally. I looked down and was startled to see that I had a chubby baby's body, about four months old! I appeared to be lying on my back, but it did not matter which way I was facing, because I was weightless — there was no gravity; I was suspended in space. There was nothing to see in any direction, but I felt safe and satisfied; this experience far excelled what I had hoped for as a response to my earnest plea for direct evidence of a spiritual nature. Was I supposed to do anything? Could I? These thoughts seemed irrelevant. There would be no way physical science could explain what had happened. I was in awe, and thinking did not feel to be as necessary as just observing.

I could see my body clearly except where my genitals should have been; that area was fuzzy and shaded with dark lines. I could see only my arms, torso, and legs distinctly, and glimpsed the edges of my eye sockets and nose. I could see that there was a faint patch of light in the far distance when I looked past my feet, but soon I noticed that the distant light was moving very slowly towards me, so I concentrated on it. A cluster of small glowing lights was travelling silently towards me — or me towards it. The light came from globes slightly larger than tennis balls. As it approached me my body gradually became bathed in soft light. Several dozen glowing balls glided very slowly around me on all sides at walking speed, passing to my rear as if directed by some intelligence. This was obviously a planned interception because the bubbles were evenly spaced, the outermost being no further than about three metres each side of my body. When I was completely illuminated, my senses suddenly shut down.

I was unaware of anything else except a feeling of deep peace. When I opened my eyes, it was morning. I was feeling very calm, refreshed, and emotionally fulfilled because my earnest spiritual enquiries had produced a result, and there was now no doubt that there were other dimensions. In later years I was to read a quote from Paramahansa Yogananda that is appropriate to mention here; recommending that you say to yourself when commencing meditation: 'I am beyond body, thought and speech.' Looking back later, I realise I must have been in such a state but decided that I should attempt to think and understand what I was experiencing. On Google, there is a dimension in Hindu philosophy described in Sanskrit as turiya, a state of wakeful sleep. Sanskrit is the language that more scriptures were written in than any other language. Turiya is the highest of the four states of consciousness. It transcends the previous three wakened states. It has been called conscious samadhi.

Had I achieved such a state?

Chapter 5
Meditation lessons

A teacher finds me

I READ AN ADVERTISEMENT IN THE LOCAL community newspaper that there would be a talk and video presentation about Sathya Sai Baba, a famous Indian man, and the venue was in the adjacent street to my flat and so I decided to attend. A small team headed by a scientist enjoyed arranging speakers to talk on health, conservation, or spiritual subjects. They advertised their talks as 'Soul's Quest'. This evening's video presentation was to be about the planning and building of a 'Super Specialty Hospital' for the Sathya Sai Baba Trust. Sathya Sai Baba was a respected spiritual leader in India whose followers had built a temple for him in an isolated desert village where he had been born, and still resided for most of the year. The hospital had been designed by architects in London to spiritual specifications and the design and building took only seven months. The money had been provided by an American who had sold his chain of businesses. He told British architects that he wanted to build a hospital in a desert village in India, a project that would normally take seven to ten years. The video producers were of the belief that the whole operation would have been impossible to complete in such a short time but for divine intervention. They considered that Sathya Sai Baba was an avatar — an incarnation of God. This evening the planning and building of the hospital appeared to be the focus of the presentation. There was no photo of Sathya Sai Baba, who was usually referred to as Sai Baba, or just Baba. I was not to know at this time that within a few years I would personally visit that hospital.

Sri Sathya Sai Super Specialty Hospital

When I entered the hall where the video presentation was to be held, I attempted to feel intuitively where to sit. Most of the casually dressed audience appeared to be in their thirties and forties. I chose a seat next to a buxom elderly woman who was unaccompanied; I felt that she may appreciate having someone to chat to.

'Hello,' I said, giving her a smile as I sat down. 'How long have you been in New Zealand?' I asked. She seemed surprised at my question and laughed as if caught off guard.

'What do you mean?' she asked me.

'Well, you are English, aren't you?' I said.

'Why do you say that?' she said. I explained how I knew: she was wearing a quality winter coat that was a necessity to keep warm in the colder northern hemisphere winter. The tilt of her head when she turned to talk to me was certainly British, as were her facial mannerisms. She had grey hair in a tidy style from an earlier era.

She laughed. She had been in New Zealand for about 40 years. She told me that her name was Joy. She avoided driving at night and did not like to drive in the rain, but it was cold and raining this evening.

'Why did you come out tonight then?' I asked.

Joy told me: 'I heard a voice telling me that I had to go to this meeting because I have to meet someone. Usually, I have to look around to see who it might be, but tonight I did not have to look. You found me instead!' she said enthusiastically.

My lifelong hope that fairy tales and religious scriptures were not the only places where amazing things happened was coming true.

'Would you like to come home with me for spiritual development?' asked Joy, after the presentation had ended. 'Would you like me to teach you spiritual healing and meditation?' I accepted her offer.

I had always wondered what meditation was and so I said yes to Joy's offer to teach me. By this stage of my life, I had become aware that for some reason my desire to find genuine spiritual teachers was finally becoming reality. I was later to learn that if a teacher's offer to teach was not accepted or perhaps not even recognised as an opportunity to advance spiritually, it could result in an opportunity missed. Joy's offer entailed some sacrifice on her part because of her age because it was after 10 pm when we left the meeting. Joy was 67 years old.

'It's only a five-minute drive to my place,' she told me. I walked home to the nearby street, collected my car, and followed Joy while she drove to her house.

Joy's tidy lounge had a dining table and chairs and a comfortable couch. There was a small telephone table covered by a cotton tablecloth with a small, framed drawing of Jesus on it. A photograph of a brown-skinned elderly man, probably an Indian, with a mop of black frizzy hair, stood beside a candle in a candleholder.

'That's Sathya Sai Baba,' she said. 'I saw him once. I was meditating and he was passing me on another path. He looked across at me and nodded.' At the presentation that we had just left, there had not been any photograph of him displayed, and the presentation was only about the hospital being constructed. This visit to Joy's house was to be the first of many.

'I go to the services at the local Anglican church most Sundays,' Joy told me over the following weeks. 'I love the choir!' She looked ecstatic at the memory. She also attended local spiritualist churches. Recently, I had heard mention of spiritualist churches. Some of the people I had recently given a tarot card reading to had asked me if I ever went to one — I knew nothing about them — but I resolved to investigate what they did at their services. Normally I would not attend any church's services.

For this first lesson, Joy demonstrated spiritual healing to me. Joy told me that the belief that I was a healer would make the healing operative, but first a prayer should be said to ask if healing, or giving the patient some relief, was permitted. Many people are unaware that they can utilise special capabilities that are beyond what is usually perceived as normal. Using intuition is necessary. When I placed my hand near various parts of Joy's body, I could feel small vibrations on my palms and sometimes I had a clammy feeling on my fingers. I saw that my fingers emitted a blue colour when I relaxed and was planning to start healing. The aim of the exercise had been to put my mind in a calm state and *believe* that I was a healer and that would allow the healing energies to flow. Rex's dowsing system at the parapsychology school had probably evolved into this type of healing.

I left Joy's home about 2 am. She appeared to be extremely pleased to be of service to me, so I agreed to return for instruction on meditation the following Saturday.

Developing a meditation technique

I was five minutes late for my appointment with Joy who was outside cheerfully watering her flower gardens. 'Come over here, David, and look at these flowers — I mean *really look*!' She emphasised her words by throwing her arms out wide in front of the flowers, as if to embrace their fragrance. 'Don't worry about the neighbours that may watching,' she insisted. 'Just enjoy the flowers. Aren't they wonderful?'

I did as she asked, but I was not a home gardener and had never been one.

'Really *look* at them!' she emphasised.

I leaned over a cluster of flowers and held one of them by its stem. As I looked intently at the stamen at the centre of the orange petals I felt as if Joy's confidence in my potential capabilities was excessive, but I wanted to demonstrate that I appreciated her efforts. Imagine my surprise when everything in the centre and around the petals started to glow until all the petals were white as if from an inner light. Around the exterior of the petals there was a blue aura.

'The petals have all lit up!' I said, obviously flabbergasted; the flower had an aura that was the complementary colour of the petals. I was to discover that this is always the case with colours — there are complementary colours that are usually unseen. There are 14 colours including the seven that are visible to everyone.

Joy was giggling, obviously pleased that I had made this discovery. I was still getting that feeling of 'Why me?' I felt rather foolish that Joy seemed to be thinking that I had special qualities, but I might soon be found to have underwhelming abilities — a spiritual fraud. Later, it occurred to me that a few centuries ago if I had told people about my experience with the flowers, poor Joy might have been accused of being a witch! She appeared ecstatic to be helping me to be aware of my psychic abilities, and to develop them, as she called it.

Soon we were comfortably seated inside. Joy propped up a large painting about two metres in front of where we sat. It showed a pathway leading away into a forest past rows of flowers on each side. Joy handed me a typewritten prayer: 'This is a prayer of protection before we start the meditation.' What do we need to be protected from? I wondered. We said the prayer together — I kept it to take home.

'The painting is to help with the meditation, but you decide what is best for you. Every person has their own individual preference. I am going to play some relaxing music now while I talk you through the meditation. Now: imagine that you are walking along that path in the painting; you may prefer to close your eyes. Try to be as comfortable as you can, so relax your arms and legs; relax the muscles in your face and in your jaw. Keep your mind as free of thoughts as you can.' She paused, as if waiting to see if I responded positively.

'Imagine that there is a closed white gate in front of you and there is a guard standing there. Ask for permission to enter. Do not enter if the gate does not open; your energy may be too low. Do not force your way in; things could go wrong for you. When the gate opens you may see people that you know greeting you. They will accompany you. Move onwards with them and walk along the path between the rows of flowers.'

As I listened to Joy talking, I tried to imagine walking along the pathway. I did my best to concentrate on moving my imaginary legs, until we eventually arrived at a temple or church after crossing a river and moving uphill on a white path. People were singing hymns as I made my way to the altar where Joy told me to light a candle. This story then had me retrace my steps to the starting point of the meditation. I opened my eyes and 20 minutes had passed.

'I feel very tired,' I said. 'I was using a lot of mental energy trying to imagine my arms and legs moving. I didn't "see" anything that you were suggesting that I see.'

'Forget about your legs and arms,' said Joy. 'You are just "travelling", but don't think about physical movement. You do not have to try to see anything. Things will just appear.'

She told me I should practise this meditation every day. She then handed me a coloured diagram of the human chakra system, the energy-psychic-spiritual system that energises the body. I made an appointment for another meditation lesson the following week. I was soon to notice that the order that the colours of the flowers beside the pathway had been listed was the same as the order that the human body's chakras were listed on the diagram that Joy had given me. Perhaps the flowers' colours prompt the mediation to have a positive result.

'Don't be late — they'll all be waiting for you!' Joy called out as I left her house. I smiled at how naturally and unselfconsciously she made that statement.

I had heard that meditation was a method to give the mind a rest from its undisciplined chattering. I was determined to make a serious effort to put the system Joy taught into practice. I decided on a time that I would set aside to practise daily, and I was to keep to that time for many months.

The following week I made sure I was on time for my second meditation lesson, which was a variation of the first one. The typed meditation was headed 'Meditation No. 2'. There would be three more weekly lessons. After the third week, I had practised Meditation Number 3, and I reported to Joy that I was puzzled. 'Joy,' I said, 'I mentally went through the meditation journey, trying to forget that I have a body. At home it took me twenty minutes for the first two weeks but after the third lesson, when I finished telling myself the story, it had taken thirty minutes. I only vaguely remembered hearing the music that I had put on to help me relax.' Was I too tired?

Joy did not offer any explanation.

We then went through Meditation Number 4 together. I told her that I still did not see images of any kind. 'You don't have to try to see anything,' Joy reminded me. I assured her that I would continue to practise daily at home. She told me that most of her pupils did not practise consistently. 'That's up to them,' Joy said. 'Some do not even complete the course of five. Sometimes they do not turn up for appointments or are late. Sometimes they bring another person with them and they giggle from time to time.'

I was genuinely surprised to hear about Joy's other pupils' lack of commitment, and apparent lack of respect for Joy. Much later, I concluded that perhaps not everyone recognised her as a genuine meditation teacher. After all, she could not give a physical demonstration that what she taught would work. Many months later, when I had gained more experience, I understood that some of the people that Joy was attempting to train may have been looking for *fast* psychic advancement. I was aware now that to aspire to be spiritual needed commitment; it takes time, diligence, and patience — and sincerity. I had thought that everyone would be like me and jump at the opportunity that Joy offered. I was certain now that a commitment to *personal* improvement was necessary. It could be that the personality had to be side-stepped to allow the true immortal ego to be revealed.

'My husband died a few years ago,' explained Joy over the next few months. 'He didn't have any interest in my spiritual life when he was alive. I used to wait until he was in bed, then I sat up meditating alone in the lounge. Each day he would call at a Masonic club on his way home from work and he went to bed soon after arriving home.'

Joy was beginning to tell me about her own personal experiences. I admit, if I had not had the earlier mention of personal spiritual help that apparently came from another sphere or level of consciousness, from real beings, or from the akashic records, I too would probably have been more sceptical. I had been prepared to wait until I had more personal experience of spiritual matters before I believed or disbelieved.

Spiritual guide and spiritual master

When I kept my appointment with Joy to teach me meditation, as arranged, she told me that her house was going to be put on the market for sale because it was too large for her, so she was soon going to be searching for a more suitable home to move to. She told me that she had some painting and tidying up to do so that the house would be more presentable for a potential buyer.

She told me that she had a spiritual 'guide' — perhaps Francie's 'Fred' had been a guide. Joy also informed me that another being had appeared to her and administered healing to her. 'I was surprised when he appeared to me one day covered with a protective suit, like armour, because he had to lower his vibrations to enter our earth's dimension. He was extremely tall — he had to bend his head down to fit in this room. However, he adjusted to our earth level of vibration after several visits and eventually didn't need the suit.' His name was Sherediona. I never thought to question Joy about whether he had materialised. I had assumed that Joy could see him with an inner eye, like the way that I could see auras. These days I wonder: was Sherediona a being from a spiritually advanced race, or planet, that was able to be projected to another location when required? Please be patient with me; this is a story that I tell just like it happened. I have always been extremely sceptical of stories about beings from other planets, and only recently had heard of guides. I did tell you that I had been determined to keep an open mind; so far this attitude has led me to many welcome surprises and heartfelt relief that we are in a universe full of hidden wonders that are basically part of nature. Joy told me that Sherediona had directed healing energy through her on a few occasions when she placed her hands on a patient.

I was introduced to Nancy, a friend of Joy's. She told me: 'I was not well one day, and I appealed to Sherediona for healing. I felt his huge hands on me. He was a wonderful healer. I called for him occasionally when I was unwell.' I was soon to meet another of Joy's friends, Marie, who confirmed Joy and Nancy's description of Sherediona.

Joy said that she had been given some help with the meditations she taught by a prompting from a master soul called White Eagle. White Eagle was a teacher from the spirit — a higher sphere or vibration — and you could say that he was with the senior management of a spiritual brotherhood. He was not a guide. I had not been told when or exactly how this intermittent assistance to Joy had started.

Joy lent me books written by an Englishwoman, Grace Cooke, who had written many books about White Eagle during the twentieth century. Grace wrote that she had relayed messages from him all her life. We should not think of him as a specific person: he is a spokesperson for the many wise ones behind him. He is quoted as saying that he is expressing the truths that they are all aware of. I looked up the name White Eagle in an encyclopaedia of mystical words; it means like an eagle that can see clearly for miles and is a name given to any spiritual teacher who discerns truth from untruth.

White Eagle, I was informed by Nancy, is the head of the White Brotherhood — the brotherhood first brought to my attention by the teachers at the parapsychology school. It has been called The Brotherhood of the Great White Light.

For years I had realised that I must strive consistently to reduce the usual ramblings of my mind. I wanted to be more receptive to the upper levels of the psychic/spiritual akasha. If I were using a radio receiver as an example, I would probably be intending to change from the AM frequency to FM, and so it was essential that I direct my thoughts to a specific goal. I would try to crystallise that goal as becoming fully intuitional. Bear in mind that I had an idea of God at this time as having an unfathomable cosmic nature that must have been the initiator and maintainer of all that we can see or imagine, including other dimensions. I did not accept that there was a Personal God, but by now I was certain that each person's aspirations were not lost among the jumble of humanity's thoughts. At the appropriate time, action would be taken to respond to these aspirations, but at our material level the result may not be what we expected.

Can I astral travel?

A curious incident happened: I chatted briefly with a young man who was about 20 years old. I was in the local library and we had exchanged some comment and so when I saw him a few weeks later walking towards me on a local street, I greeted him. The young man acknowledged me but gave me a wide berth and kept walking. 'Is there something wrong?' I blurted out.

'You were in my home last night,' he said as he walked purposefully away.

'What do you mean?' I called after him. 'I don't know where you live.'

'I saw you in my house!' he said emphatically.

Was it possible that I had visited him in my astral body? That seemed unlikely, but how else could I have been in his house? Was I capable of doing that unconsciously? It did seem to be a meaningless exercise if I had; it was rather spooky too. A humorous thought entered my mind: would I need an alibi if the young man reported me to the police for trespassing — if they could locate me?

During the years ahead I would meet people who would help me to understand more about psychic and spiritual experiences. Some of them have remained my spiritual confidants and true friends until the present day.

By now I was convinced that everyone with the correct sincerity and application would find the key to truth. There was no locked door to understanding, but, in my opinion, love and discrimination were required. Sages throughout history must have known that it was necessary for each person to apply what wisdom they were given to their own circumstances. There are natural laws that must be applied, and everyone could be living in harmony if these laws were obeyed.

Chapter 6
Symbolic images

Magic in the sun

I DECIDED TO TRY A NEW METHOD OF SEEING AURAS one sunny morning. I looked at the reflection of my face in the large mirror in my bathroom for 20 seconds or so, trying not to think or blink, then promptly shut my eyes to see what would happen. About 15 seconds later I was surprised when my face appeared, but it was completely orange. This image kept returning and gradually fading until after a few minutes it had shrunk into a blob and almost disappeared — and I still had my eyes closed!

The next day, when I repeated the same experiment in the bathroom, no colours appeared in my inner eye. This puzzled me until I remembered that the day before had been a bright sunny day and today was partly cloudy. And so perhaps I needed more light to improve the chances of success with my experiment. The bathroom window had only one small window to let the light in, so I went outside and looked directly at the source of the light — the sun. Why I had this notion, which realistically was foolhardy, I will never know. When I had given my full attention to focusing on the flower petal in Joy's garden, I had achieved amazing results; it was worth trying the same technique.

I stared straight at the sun without blinking, for what I had predetermined should be only one and a half seconds, because I did not want to be completely reckless. It was extremely difficult to stay focused because the sun was blindingly strong, as expected; it was like staring at a welding flame. A perfectly round thin black line that could have been drawn by a compass enclosed the blinding white light. I closed my eyes and waited.

After the usual 15 or 20 seconds passed waiting for a response, I was gratified to see a bluish-green circular image appear, surrounded by a greenish-yellow aura. The image kept fading every 10 or 15 seconds or so, then returning. The shape of the image kept changing and so did the colours. At first the image divided into two round circles, but then one circle had become smaller each time it reappeared until it had totally disappeared, leaving only one patch of colour, which was now gold. It then gradually formed into the shape of a gold-coloured vessel, very slightly oblong in shape. It was not clearly defined — the extremities were blurred. After a while it had become red, and then the colour faded and disappeared. I was astonished! A woman acquaintance had told me one year earlier that a gold cup had appeared to her while she was driving her car, supposedly with her eyes wide open. All the while my eyes had remained closed.

The next day I was intrigued enough to attempt to see the cup again, and my eyes had not noticeably deteriorated, so I —

perhaps foolishly — repeated the experiment. The sun image that appeared to my inner sight again split into two separate blobs. They were a greenish-yellow colour, but each blob became taller and developed into two hooded images of monks. They faced each other, side on to my viewing point. They appeared to be composed of a marble-like material, were overly tall and obviously stylised. Their cassocks fully covered their limbs. One of them gradually became green and the other one blue. The green monk gradually grew taller with each changing scene and the blue monk kept reducing in size, but then both finally shrank into coloured blobs again as the intensity of the colours dissipated. After about four minutes, only a faint remnant of colour remained.

The images of monks were extremely clear and detailed, as if I could reach out and hold them. The gold cup had been indistinct. I repeated this experiment again a few days later, not sure what to expect. This time, I saw a crystal-clear image of hearts! Later I did my best to draw them with a coloured pencil set that I had purchased for use at the colour therapy classes. The hearts were a set of three, each drawn as a single line — a red heart was in the centre with a blue one encircling it. Around the outside of both was a violet heart. This image kept to the same rhythm as in my previous experiments with aura colours — it faded and then reappeared — but the hearts were changing their position with each fresh appearance. They gradually slanted towards the right, the red one being on the left end and the violet one on the right end, with the blue one in between, and there was a space separating each one. As they tilted, I could see that I was being shown a representation of a net like a butterfly net, with the red heart at the bottom. When they reached a 45-degree angle I could still see them perfectly clearly, but then the scene gradually faded with each pulsation. It was obvious that through my eyes, every image that I saw had been because my brain had been stimulated by the influence of the light of the sun.

The three hearts apparitions brought my attention to the importance of light. It was obvious that without the light, from the sun in this case, I would have no result. I wondered what would happen if I used another source of light. I soon found that if I focused on a strong light globe, I would again have an apparition of three hearts coloured the same as previously, but each time I repeated this exercise I had a completely new pattern of hearts. For example, one set looked as if each heart was made of coloured glass or precious stones and another set had a plastic-like appearance. It always seemed as if I should be able to reach out and grasp them. For reasons that I do not know, I continued to have only visions of hearts after staring at bright lights.

One of the best psychics that I was ever to meet, later explained to me that my vision of a gold cup represents 'the cup of knowledge for life'. She told me that gold represents heart wisdom. This interpretation was confirmed in later years by other clairvoyants.

A few weeks later I moved to live at a friend's house as a house-sitter while she went overseas. When she returned, after an absence of several weeks, I continued to live there. One night I had a dream in which the three hearts were a simple outline as if drawn by coloured pencils. The outer line was violet as usual, shown as a faded *dotted* line that was not a uniform distance from the edge of the blue heart. That indicated to me that I was uncomfortable with my situation where I was living at the time. My kind friend who owned the house had started hosting a group of enthusiastic people who met every evening, hoping to fast-track their spiritual development by using what I felt were dogmatic methods that I did not feel in harmony with. My friend had a special talent for getting people together, but I was certain that their system was not the way for me to proceed, so I excused myself and continued with my meditations, which were now conducted every evening at 7 pm. I moved to new accommodation several weeks later.

The heart visions and aura interests gradually faded over the next three years. It would have been wiser to look at the sun when it was obscured, therefore filtered, by a cloud, and less dangerous to the eyes, but the sun would have to be looked at for a longer period because of the lower light intensity. Perhaps there is a spiritual sun co-existing with the physical sun. The sun worshippers of various cultures in the past possibly had some experiences like mine. In India, the word for sun in ancient classical Sanskrit is Surya, a deity.

Tarot card practice

I had spent hours each week trying to perfect my tarot card readings, without success. When I did not develop more natural intuitional insight into the meanings that the cards were representing, I concluded that perhaps I was probably not going to improve, so I reduced my practice time drastically.

Francie and Dean had taught that when people use cards, the images trigger psychic responses within the reader. They had told me to shuffle until I felt that I should stop, and then examine the cards. However, I did not get any special urge to stop, but whatever I did there was usually a remarkable reading.

When I had attended Francie's school she had been pleased with my results and appeared to think that I had a special gift, but the intensive practice that I had been doing for months did not give me the *natural* insight that excellent tarot readers had. As far as I knew, some card readers had not received any special instruction at a school. They must have been naturally psychic. Maybe I was not suited to be an expert at tarot cards. I needed more clarity about what is psychic and what is spiritual.

I had been giving tarot card readings for several people every week but became concerned when I could not read accurately enough to give the information that some of them were hoping for. Some people had serious problems. For example: 'Should I leave my husband? He is having an affair!' Or, when it appeared obvious that a woman had two lovers who wanted to marry her, which one should she choose? It appeared to me that one was obviously carrying out illegal activities; the client agreed with me that he was a criminal. I could not do anything other than hand the responsibility for such a critical decision back to the enquirer, although I could describe the conditions within the relationships. I did, however, ask the woman dating the criminal if she had thought about what her children's life would be like, if she planned to have any, if she chose the criminal to be her permanent partner. She appeared to be troubled when she left.

I stopped giving readings except when they were requested by acquaintances. Quite often it would be for a person who had psychic ability who wanted confirmation of what they already knew. Some of them would then give me their psychic impressions about my own circumstances. For example, 'Are you living in a suitcase?' At the time, I was living in the tiny room at my friend's house. I realised that spending a lot of time practising with the tarot cards had kept me from other activities. I had a half-metre-high pile of paper that I had written my practice readings on. I started to socialise more and get out among nature more often, as I was often advised to do, otherwise I felt unfocused.

I wondered about the power of thought. Did I have to write down a question before I laid out the tarot cards? I tried thinking the question and was not surprised when of course that produced results too, rather like the random choice of books. Because every word used to formulate the question influences what cards are displayed, it is important to remember the *exact* question! Keeping a note of it is more accurate.

Rather like a library or the internet, it was necessary to know exactly how to word any query so that you get the answers that you require. Francie had told her class that if you do not get the answer that you expect, it is no use pushing for a more acceptable answer because you only receive the answer that you are permitted — or deserve — to get.

The tarot card practice that I was doing did not seem to be making me more sensitive psychically. It was time to broaden the scope of my investigations and experiments, and to improve my social life.

A symbolic dream

About this time, I had a long dream that was especially intriguing. It was not perfectly clear like the babe in the light lucid dream because it was quite fuzzy like an average dream. When the dream started, I was driving alone along a road that had little traffic. There were low hills. I turned right to enter a large property enclosed by a fence. There were a dozen or so tiny wooden unpainted buildings evenly scattered about. I stopped at a small shop on the property and bought something and then continued to drive past the huts. When I parked by a beach a man was fishing with a rod to my left. I took a fishing rod from my car and cast a line into the water and immediately had a continuous pull on the line. I had caught a small fish. I heard a man's voice in the background shout out a strange word. I do not recall anything else after that except being surprised and thrilled with my catch. When I woke up, I drew a rough sketch of the scene as I remembered it, including the fish. I wrote down the shouted word, 'Ngunguru'. I guessed that it was probably a Maori word.

About five years later, a man was fronting a TV documentary that was screening. The presenter was travelling around the coast of New Zealand by various ships. I was suddenly alert because I heard the word 'Ngunguru'. I consulted a map: Ngunguru was a township 28 kilometres northeast of Whangarei, which was almost a three-hour drive north of Auckland. I travelled there from Hamilton with a friend several weeks later. Everything that was in the dream was there in actuality, but the tiny unpainted buildings were in fact small, one-bedroom cottages, in a holiday camp. There seemed to be no obvious reason why a real place I had never been should have been presented to me in a dream.

Chapter 7
Experiences in spiritualist churches

I WAS OFTEN ASKED BY THE PEOPLE THAT I HAD READ tarot cards for if I had ever been to a spiritualist church. Out of curiosity I started to attend several churches regularly and continued to do so for the next seven years. In a spiritualist church the word 'spirit' was the word usually used by spiritualists to describe any spiritual/psychic agencies. There was always an invited medium or a person with some special psychic or spiritual capability, such as clairvoyance, who would give a short talk followed by a demonstration which was intended to prove the continuation of the human spirit after death. There was no talk about sinners, Satan, or damnation in Hell. Jesus was an exemplar, not a saviour. Viewing these events proved to be an interesting learning curve for me. Over time I began to understand the different capabilities that each presenter had, and I discovered that many people in the congregation had some psychic ability. When I observed the speakers' demonstrations, I noticed their different psychic-spiritual qualities. Just like there are different cloud layers in the sky; some are many thousands of feet up, and some scrape the hilltops. No one seemed to mind if another person's personal spiritual interest was unorthodox.

At my first attendance at a spiritualist church, I was surprised to see Joy there. She told me that she had already been to the Anglican service in the city's cathedral and hurried along to this service as soon as the Anglican one finished. The medium 'on the platform' —there being no pulpit or altar — was introduced to the congregation.

'Good morning, everyone,' she said. 'My guide told me that it's important that he give the address today. Please be patient.' The medium was an elegantly dressed pleasant-looking woman about 40 years old. She relaxed briefly with her eyes closed, and then I was astonished when she delivered a profound speech without any pauses to organise her words. I was amazed by the wise sentiments expressed and by the confident manner that the talk was delivered in. The talk was all about the brotherhood of mankind, harmony, love, and forgiveness. What intrigued me was the personality revealed in her voice.

'I think that was White Eagle speaking through the medium today,' Joy said. 'He does that, you know.'

No, I had not known. I was to find out that White Eagle is apparently available anywhere if the need is present, but only if there is a suitable channel. In one of the books containing his quotes that Joy had lent me, he said that if there is a need for important information to be passed on, the most appropriate channel available is utilised, even if the channel is not as pure as he would like.

She had no hesitation about telling the Anglicans at the cathedral what she experienced in her meditations, and any other spiritual information that she thought would benefit them. She had no fear of whether they scoffed or not, and they in their turn must have at least tolerated her. She usually had a huge smile on her face when she was talking. She was a very forthright person and this characteristic caused her to occasionally have quite forceful disagreements with some of the members of the church when she felt certain that she was correct.

I began to attend two spiritualist churches that meet on alternate weeks. During my sixth attendance, a medium on the platform asked me if she could come to me. I agreed that she could. 'A lady sends you a lot of love,' she told me. 'She's giving you a gigantic bunch of flowers. She is concerned that you are spending too much time on your own, deep thinking, but you need to get out and talk to other people. The lady is short and slim but put on weight around the middle as she got older. Originally, she came from a long distance away overseas.' Similar advice was to be given to me regularly by mediums over the next few years. The description given fitted my deceased stepmother who had been born in England but immigrated to New Zealand when she was a teenager. She had died four years earlier.

These messages indicated that I was still studying excessively. Maybe a lot of book study was not helping my spiritual progress. I am not a scholar; and besides, I tended to get sleepy when I studied — I am a browser really. By luck I often seemed to find a few pages in a book that have just the information I needed to clarify some quandary that I had or save me from possible disaster. Twelve years later, after I retired, I spent considerable time immersed in many books but had no trouble maintaining focus because by then I was soaking in Indian and

Far Eastern philosophy that provided answers to mystical queries that had puzzled me.

Some mediums say that they see a person in spirit that wants to pass on a message, and some mediums give out names when they pass on messages. I have observed mediums that gave out a name or a description and then asked if anyone knew them.

The mediums gave me encouraging messages that they said were from my grandfather on about five occasions over the next several years. The first two times he was alone, then the next three times he said that he had my father with him. At first, I was puzzled, because if my father was with him three times, why was my grandfather giving the message each time? A year passed after the fifth message. At last, a medium said to me: 'Your father's here. He says that there is a job coming up for you. "There's plenty of life in the old fellow yet!" he says.' I did not have paid employment at this time but had two volunteering jobs. About two years after that last message, I started a very satisfying job.

I eventually had a more heartfelt message: 'Your father's here,' a medium told me. 'He said that he is sorry that he wasn't the father that you would have wanted. He kept to himself because he had his own problems. He is proud of you.'

Joy displayed a stubborn streak at church one day. Mediums are trained to ask permission to come to the person that the message is intended for. Joy told me that several years after her husband had died, he had tagged along behind another person in spirit. Joy had stubbornly refused to accept the message from the medium because her husband had not come forward by himself; she considered that he was avoiding 'talking' to her directly. Many months later I was sitting with her, when a medium told her that once again her husband was there but wanted to have his message passed on by a person who was with him.

'May I come to you? Your husband is here with a friend,' the medium asked.

'No,' said Joy, as she giggled nervously. She had a determined look on her face. The medium hesitated but collected her wits and moved on to continue dispensing messages.

'He has to have the courage to come forward himself,' Joy muttered to me, as if she expected me to understand. Later she informed me: 'He left me in a mess financially when he died. I had to get paid work to pay off debts. He didn't discuss anything financial with me when he was alive.'

I was present about two years later when Joy was finally satisfied. A medium told her that her husband had come forward alone and apologised for leaving her with serious problems. Over the seven years that I attended spiritualist churches I received more than 200 messages from various relatives and others.

'Feeling' for the truth

I introduced myself to Mark, a tall man who had been on the platform at the spiritualist church sometimes, and later we became friends. I had been impressed with his calm and thoughtful demeanour. He could channel information — he could often be observed in conversation with someone passing on information that he apparently had received clairvoyantly. He often went within — thought deeply — to check on the correctness of another person's opinion, including finding a truthful reply to a question. I asked him if I could learn how to do this. A few weeks later he told me that I was ready to channel. I joined a spiritual development class that he supervised. However, what I had gradually unfolded within myself later was not what I had anticipated as channelling. Mark had a remarkable attribute: he would put his hand on a book and know whether it was worthwhile for him to read it. He preferred to learn by experience and by going within, as some psychics describe it, and he told me that he rarely read a book.

By now I was certain that the psychological conditions described as psychic and spiritual were not the same but were part of the combination of factors that combine to make a human being. To be truly spiritual, there was no escaping the necessity to strive to be the best person possible — in *deed and thought*. It was necessary to develop a non-judgmental and non-materialistic attitude, and it had to become permanent. Mark was a man that I considered to have that attitude. To this day he is a reliable friend.

Joy's back story

'My husband thought that I caused unnecessary trouble,' Joy told me. Despite numerous requests, a neighbour had not trimmed the overhanging branches of a tree that hung too far over an adjoining fence, and so Joy had trimmed the tree and thrown the cuttings onto the neighbour's lawn.

She was a person with great integrity who had worked for various charities when she was younger. She told me that her guide had told her never to get on a committee or be involved in anything political. I could see the wisdom of this advice because it was obvious that she was not going to compromise over anything when she had concluded that her view was correct. Unfortunately, it turned out that she could be gullible because she had helped people who were not honest, and so got herself into difficulties. She had considered that the nice man that she visited in jail deserved her friendship, but he had lied to her: he was not in jail for lax paperwork regarding taxes, as he had told her at church prior to being sentenced — he was a convicted child molester.

Joy's husband had been admitted to hospital when he was seriously ill. Whenever he had been unwell, he had always refused to go to a doctor, but this time it became obvious that he was not going to be returning home although he was only 63 years old.

'When I was visiting him at the hospital, he was trying to get out of bed but was connected to all the medical wires and tubes,' said Joy. She asked him what he was trying to do.

'I'm trying to get up that white pole,' he said, but there was no white pole visible. He died soon afterwards.

Am I unconscious?

Three weeks after I started practising meditation daily there had been a very peculiar development. 'I am still having difficulties with the meditation you taught me,' I told Joy. 'I sit down on my couch and get some pillows to support my head. If I do not do that, when I finish the meditation, my head has dropped down to one side and my neck is very stiff. I have not visualised anything, but I was not aware of my surroundings for about forty minutes. What do you think has happened?'

Joy had no explanation but did not seem concerned. I continued to go to her home for instruction, but she told me that I had finished her course when we completed Meditation Number 5; it was up to me to continue to practise.

A clear pattern had eventually become established. I would commence my usual meditation routine: I would get comfortable and then take deep breaths, which was a trigger to instigate a change in my consciousness. Pale-yellow 'doughnuts' like smoke rings would start to float past from behind after encircling me. Everything exterior to me faded away unobtrusively as if I were falling asleep. Eventually, when I regained my usual consciousness, I would find that an hour had passed, my throat would be dry, I would feel groggy, and it would take me 10 minutes to recover.

Rescue work

Over the following months Joy told me some of the interesting things that had happened to her during her meditations. People she knew accompanied her and they crossed over a river via a bridge, then they passed a colourful row of flowers — the colours were carefully noted in a certain order — and went up a white path to a temple or church, where Joy lit a candle; she then returned the way that she came, thanking anyone who escorted her.

'If you see people you know when you are on the way up to the higher paths who seem surprised to see you, tell them "Hello" and that you are still alive on the physical plane; you have not died yet, but keep on going up the path. *Never* leave the white path.'

This, of course, is all symbolic, but apparently some meditation students do see paths and people, but I did not.

What was the rescue work? I had previously heard that terminology. As Joy travelled up the path, she would often see someone who was off to one side struggling to get onto the path. 'I would say things like "Come on! You can do it. Come here and get onto the path with me." Sometimes it took a determined effort from them.' She told me that she would not get off the path to help them or she risked disaster for herself. If any person she saw did not try, she would have to leave them. 'Some of the figures who were struggling to move or were prostrate were looking as if they needed me to go and help them; some even called out for assistance, but they were not all innocent; they could cause harm to me or anyone leaving the path.

'I once saw golden steps leading to a temple near the end of my outward journey and was surprised to see that there was a nun lying collapsed by the bottom step. I encouraged her to get up but would not help even when she pleaded with me, but I did escort her up to the altar inside the temple. I then insisted that the nun make a determined effort to light the candle there. She suddenly swung around and snarled at me! She looked like a demon! She had no intention of lighting the candle. Then she vanished.

'You have to give the souls that aren't on the white path encouragement to make more effort to go "to the light". They must make the decision themselves. You can't help them or force them,' said Joy.

The souls that Joy rescued disappeared after they lit the candle because they were released to a higher spiritual state — the flame symbolises divinity.

Joy told me how she had been offered the opportunity to 'develop' years before: 'I heard a voice say, "Do you want to be psychic or spiritual?" So, I asked, "How long will it take?" The answer came: "Three years for psychic or seven years for spiritual." I said, "Spiritual please."'

Joy's stories were like stories that might be told to little children about a world of make-believe. Somehow, I kept an open mind, and in the following 21 or so years I patiently persisted with my spiritual studies.

Joy had been offered an opportunity for spiritual growth — she had not asked for it directly. A spiritual aspirant yearning persistently for a way forward will be offered assistance from a higher spiritual realm, but the aspirant must accept the offer — it is of no use to receive the offer and then not apply the advice offered. This means, as explained in the Dion Fortune book that I had read, a spiritual master will meet you as you climb the consciousness mountain. This information rang true for me; I was sure that it was a matter of natural law. It must be the teacher's service and part of a spiritual plan, but it is a requirement that *a teacher must be met at least halfway*. In later years I discovered that the reason was that it was a matter of natural psycho/spiritual attraction — not a decision made by a human being. After the student has remained consistently aspiring, assistance will be provided from a spiritual dimension. By now I had a vague idea of what was required to be enabled to transcend to a higher consciousness.

Often Joy would talk about her elderly friend Marie. She told me that White Eagle had been Marie's constant unseen companion all her life. He would use Marie as a compatible channel to pass on his teachings. Joy had been present when Marie, in her younger days, had regular gatherings of people at her house, some of whom had travelled from other towns. They met to hear White Eagle give spiritual talks through Marie as the instrument. Joy said that Marie had also had tuition from Sathya Sai Baba. He taught her how to look around inside people's bodies to investigate the reason for their ill health! She was made aware if she would be permitted to heal them — or not.

Chapter 8
Master Soul White Eagle

I am 'attuned'

A FEW WEEKS LATER JOY SURPRISED ME. SHE SAID: 'Marie wants to meet you. I am meeting her at a shopping mall for lunch on Saturday. Would you like to come?' Of course, I agreed wholeheartedly.

I was often embarrassed by the extravagant attention that Joy was still giving me. At spiritualist churches, she gushingly introduced me to people as if I was a special discovery. However, I did not want to miss an opportunity to meet Marie. I hoped I would not disappoint her.

Joy drove me to meet Marie at the mall on the following Saturday. Marie was a short, slightly built, grey-haired woman in her sixties with a gentle demeanour. She smiled radiantly as she greeted us. She gave each of us a friendly hug; I was surprised that she was so unassuming and humble and spoke very softly. I was a little disappointed at her appearance — she wore baggy grey track pants and training shoes; there was no attempt at glamour. However, she was dressed like many of the other shoppers. There was no hint that she was privy to any sort of spiritual knowledge.

Joy managed to say 'David does tarot ...' before Marie gently but firmly interrupted: 'White Eagle told me he knows about David. He is going to come through you today, David, so just relax and don't worry.' We chatted briefly before I heard Marie say, 'It is I, White Eagle, David. I want to talk through you today.' Joy kept enthusiastically making suggestions as to what we could do. She seemed to be unaware that it was appropriate that she let Marie control the conversation today.

I had been taken aback by Marie's unexpected comments almost immediately after our introduction, so was feeling apprehensive. She patiently insisted that we would have to find somewhere quieter. 'Maybe we should leave the mall,' I said. 'Would you like to come to my place?' Both women agreed. They chose some food in the mall to take home, and Marie paid for it. 'White Eagle told me that I should pay for lunch today,' she said.

I had to direct Marie to my flat, so I travelled with her. Marie had put a steering lock on her car. I asked her why, because surely, she was spiritually protected? 'White Eagle told me that in these troubled times it is wise to take precautions,' she answered. I wanted to hurry inside first to tidy up when we reached home, because the dining table had papers all over it, but Marie said, 'Don't worry,' so I felt quite comfortable to show her inside. Joy arrived, and Marie started to hurry around preparing the food to eat. Unexpectedly, it appeared that White Eagle spoke through her, saying, 'Just put the refreshments on the table in the bags and let everybody help themselves. Marie needs to rest.' Marie immediately relaxed, and we placed the food on the table. Later Joy told me that White Eagle always used the word refreshments for food and drink.

Joy left the table when she finished eating and moved away to the kitchen area and bustled around. When we had finished eating, White Eagle spoke again: 'David, your work will change. You will be working in a different area. You are going to be giving a different sort of reading. Your consciousness is being raised.' This eventuated — about two years later.

I was feeling nervous because there seemed to be an over-emphasis on any psychic or spiritual potential that I may have. I never considered that by work White Eagle may have meant paid employment.

The events of the day seemed like a dream.

As soon as we had all finished eating and Joy started to chat, White Eagle intervened: 'David, would you please give Marie and then Joy a reading?' It was not really a question; the words were calm but compelling.

Marie seemed quietly appreciative when I gave her a tarot card reading as diplomatically as I could, because I found it hard to believe that the cards that I had laid out could be correct. I was very self-conscious. Was I interpreting them correctly? The cards showed serious health problems. However, Marie said that she knew exactly what I meant — she had to slow down. She said that she had asked if she should pay me! The answer was no, she said. I had not given a thought to any payment.

'Now, David.' This seemed to be White Eagle speaking. It was fascinating to hear White Eagle's firm but gentle style of speaking like a very patient teacher, but Marie's mouth saying the words. 'I want you to relax and close your eyes and think of a pool of calm water. When you are ready, you may slip into the water. There is a waterfall nearby, and you may, if you want to, go under it for as long as you wish, and come out from it when you feel it is time.' I did my best to follow these instructions. After about two minutes, nothing extraordinary seemed to have happened.

At this point Joy intervened, whispering that I do not see anything when I attempt to visualise. I had briefly considered making a similar comment but decided against it — I needed to keep my mind as still as I could and surely White Eagle must already know my limitations. He responded to Joy: 'Leave him.' After about another minute, Joy was whispering again: 'I think he's asleep.' Another minute or two passed before White Eagle said, 'David, come back now.' I opened my eyes. Apart from a slight warming of my heart area, nothing dramatic seemed to have happened. I was feeling that maybe I had let my friends down and wasted their time, but then White Eagle said: 'I have achieved what I wanted, and all is well. I have attuned myself to you. Stay calm and relaxed, David, and do not worry about anything.'

Marie, apparently herself again, said, 'When you want him, White Eagle will come.'

'I can use you very well. Lead a quiet life.' These were White Eagle's final words of advice to me.

'He never said those things to me,' said Joy later when Marie was out of earshot. She sounded disappointed, but I hoped that she was not resentful. Marie and Joy stood near the front door chatting with me when it was time for them to depart.

'I'm being withdrawn from contact with people,' said Marie in her very gentle voice. 'I'm becoming too sensitive, and I'm not well. I had cancer of the stomach diagnosed by doctors and Sai Baba came and operated on me. He cut me open and inserted vibhuti [Indian sacred ash] inside,' she said very simply. 'When I saw the doctor again there was no cancer. The doctor asked me why I was there.'

Joy started to give Marie directions on how to get home from my place, because Marie had said that she had not driven so far for ages and was nervous about driving. White Eagle surprised me by talking through Marie once more: 'I have always got Marie home before, and I will get her home safely again.'

My neighbour receives a healing

Just as the women were about to leave there was a knock at the door. It was Ben, a neighbour. He was a tall man, 28 years old, with a powerful physique. He was barefoot as usual. He had previously told me that he had serious psychological problems, but he took prescription medication to keep mentally stable. He expected that some people would find his appearance intimidating. Often, he would come and talk to me when he was puzzled or angry, because he was troubled by confusing thoughts. He said that he did not know what God's purpose for him was. I had found him to be extremely intelligent, but obviously mentally unstable, although most days he was thoughtful and composed. He had great difficulty formulating his flashes of inspiration, which often led to a jumble of interesting revelations that had no cohesion that I could understand. However, he never gave up trying to decipher his disordered thoughts. He was always sincerely attempting to solve some philosophical or scientific riddle.

He had informed me that the police had shot him in the head several years earlier. He explained to me that he had a history of hallucinating and he had been waving a sword around at his family home and his mother had felt threatened. The day that he was shot he had meant no harm but admitted that if he had taken the medication prescribed for him the incident would not have happened. His mother and her partner could not cope with his unpredictable behaviour, so now he lived alone in a building adjacent to mine. He never made any attempt at housework, and so a peek inside his flat revealed what appeared to be a derelict room, with yellowed walls from cigarette smoke. On his confused days he would usually calm down after I did my best to give him a satisfactory answer to his questions, which were often of a metaphysical nature.

Today he looked as if he was desperate for a chat, but he must have been surprised to find that I had two elderly women visitors, and so he stood at the door hesitantly — I knew that he wanted immediate answers to some troubling problem. I introduced him to the two women. Without hesitation, Marie welcomed him with a beaming smile and commented that she admired his hair. She stepped forward and gave him a firm hug, which she did not immediately release. Looking bewildered, Ben responded by draping his arms carefully around her as she reached up and gently touched his hair. 'You have lovely hair,' she commented as she looked up at him. Marie took a step back, because Joy, smiling and laughing, asked Ben if she could have a hug too. She moved forward and confidently put her arms around him.

As I showed Marie out, she unobtrusively told me that she would send Ben healing later even though I had not told her anything about Ben's mental problems. She then left for home, while Joy remained and had an animated discussion with Ben for about 20 minutes about his troublesome thoughts. Joy later told me that her guide had aided her with the correct responses to give to Ben, otherwise she would have struggled to satisfy him. She was firing back immediate answers to Ben's demanding questions and appeared happy to be able to help.

After Joy had departed, Ben told me that he was amazed at the women's actions, as he was sure that most people would look at him and think that he could be dangerous. One month later, Ben came knocking again. As soon as I opened the door, he quickly walked straight inside without being invited and immediately sat down on a nearby chair. He looked rattled. 'My brain is being operated on!' he blurted out. He did not seem to be angry, but he looked perplexed. I immediately thought of Marie and her comment that she would send Ben healing later.

'What do you mean?' I said, trying to sound innocent.

'Someone is chiselling inside my head!' he said, sounding exasperated. Now I was feeling a sense of wonder — this really must have been the remote healing by Marie that she had been taught by the Indian spiritual leader Sathya Sai Baba.

What could I say? I parried his questions for a few minutes and tried to settle him down. Then he abruptly stood up and plodded off home, still looking frustrated. A few days later I was outside when he walked past and calmly told me that the chiselling had eased off. White Eagle was soon to give me some more advice.

A 'meeting' with White Eagle

Some weeks later, Joy and I were at Marie's house with other visitors, including Nancy. Joy had been planning to sell her house because it was too large for her, and today she mentioned that she was wondering when she would find a suitable property to move to. White Eagle unexpectedly began to talk through Marie.

'It is I, White Eagle. David, Marie is tired. Would you please give her healing?'

I proceeded as requested. When I had finished a few minutes later Marie thanked me, and said she now had more energy. Then White Eagle spoke again: 'We had a house for you to move to Joy. We told you to put your house on the market, but you insisted on doing some painting and this caused a delay. This extra work was not necessary. You missed the house that we had waiting for you. Never mind, because we will have another one for you when you sell this one.' This did not seem to me to be intended as a reprimand, but more as a comment on Joy's situation.

'All of you are not to worry about your spiritual progress. Be aware that Marie needs rest for her health and spiritual development. David, your meditations will improve. Do not be too soft with people. Beware giving and trusting too much.'

When Joy left the room for a few minutes, Marie told us that White Eagle is with most of our little group. We are a spiritual unit wherein each one of us assists or retards the group's spiritual advancement. Marie named seven people who formed the spiritual unit, including Nancy and her two teenage children. Joy was not named. When Joy had told me that her method of meditation had been devised with the assistance of White Eagle, he had not confirmed that her meditation was endorsed by him.

I was to become aware over the following years that when Marie said that she was very tired I was not to expect any White Eagle messages. However, White Eagle almost always had a few helpful words for me through Marie. She was to live for another 18 years.

It was on this visit that Marie handed me a book about Sathya Sai Baba's life that she said he had asked her to pass on to me. She appeared to be sad; she told me several times that she was uncomfortable with what was said to Joy through her by White Eagle. She felt responsible for upsetting Joy and never wanted it to happen again.

It eventuated that Joy must have been *terribly upset*. She never admitted it to me, but over the next few years she always politely declined any invitation from Marie to visit her. They were never to meet again. Very soon after our visit, Joy's house sold, and she easily found a property that she was happy with. However, in hindsight, Joy's mental state had started to deteriorate. She lived to be 75 years old.

Meditation problems; a new teacher channels information

I had been having difficulties during meditation. After several months persistently using the method that Joy had taught me, my thighs became so painfully cold during the meditation that they felt as if they were freezing. I started turning on an electric heater and placing a blanket over my legs before I commenced meditating. I was vaguely aware that the coldness was painful. Each time I finished; it took 20 minutes to regain normal feeling in my thighs.

This happened over 20 years ago. Was the freezing effect because my body's energy centres were being adapted for some purpose to come? Over the following three months the effect gradually reduced, and the meditation time also reduced from one hour to 30 minutes, then within weeks it became difficult for me to meditate at all using this system, but I did continue with it intermittently with mixed results; for some reason I usually could not see any yellow doughnuts. Eventually weeks elapsed between my attempts. I consulted Joy about my meditation difficulties.

'I think that you should speak to Peter; he may be able to answer your questions,' she advised me, then she gave me his telephone number. Who was Peter?

Joy and I had developed a special friendship — she occasionally made me afternoon tea at her house. She had a few eccentricities, but I was quite prepared to accept her as she was. I was hoping that I would eventually hear or see a teacher or a guide from another dimension if I patiently applied Joy's methods. I wanted to have a personal experience.

By now I knew that I would prefer to be spiritually wise rather than to have only psychic ability. I had a strong belief that releasing true wisdom from within was possible. I was certain that the source from which personal questions may be answered would have to be a psychic-spiritual bank in an accessible dimension, but certain personal qualities were essential before access was possible. There must be nature's regulations. I recalled that White Eagle had said that I should live quietly and not be concerned about spiritual progress. This must indicate that progress comes, without asking, to people who are persistent in working towards obtaining purity of the consciousness.

I spoke to Peter, the teacher recommended by Joy. I had been apprehensive about phoning him; what could he do? He may consider me a screwball. After an introductory telephone call, I met with Peter at his home. He was a fair-haired man in his forties, with a pleasant, thoughtful appearance. I told him that I vaguely felt that something was happening when I seemed to be unconscious. Peter listened attentively to me while I related my experiences; I wondered if he thought that I was attention-seeking. I was aware that my story would sound bizarre to the average person, but Peter started to respond to my knotty queries as if he could access an unlimited supply of relevant information.

'Your guides and mine say that you are being taken into the astral to a beautiful place, and all is well. You need what you are getting — your consciousness is being raised. You *are* learning something,' he said. 'You have been meditating "out of body". This is probably the most suitable method for you at this point of your development. Your guides are aware of what needs to be done for you and will use the most appropriate method, but all is within the laws of God — everything comes from God.'

Years later I arrived at the conclusion that instead of a Personal God, there were immutable Laws of Nature that cannot be avoided. It is fruitless trying to fathom how the universe started or if it has always been here with no beginning — or end. But it was becoming clear to me that God cannot communicate except through his, or her, agents.

I noticed that when I asked a question, there was a change in Peter's manner and tone of voice, and he started to speak in a measured, very assured way. Whatever question I asked him, he looked very thoughtful, as if trying to remember a telephone number.

Peter told me, 'God is *beyond* vibration.' That statement gave me food for thought for a long time. I had read a passage from a Sathya Sai Baba book that was relevant: 'God has no desire. He has no preferences and prejudices. His is but reaction, reflection and resound.' I understood that everyone is responsible for what happens in the world. 'All geology and all life are a continual reordering of the same atomic ingredients.'

'It is God's illusion, not ours,' Peter said, referring to the world that we live in. 'We are in that illusion. Illusion exists, but it is not what it appears to be. It is a wrong perception or belief.' He continued, 'Pray. Say: "Please, God, may I have a master saviour?"' I had to wonder: what does that really mean? 'Nurture love for Father and the guru,' said Peter. This must mean that he considers that a genuine guru works in harmony with God. (A guru is a spiritual master — a preceptor.) 'Work in spirit but use physical senses. Use the power of feeling — *do not read too much*. Be in harmony with the light within. We will look at things in a new way.' I have since spent hundreds of hours mulling over these words trying to grasp their full significance. They had the ring of truth. Bear in mind that this information was given to me about 22 years ago, and I have since had many almost unbelievable experiences, but it is not possible to know precisely what knowledge registered with my subconscious enough to effect a change either psychically or spiritually.

Peter often appeared to be in a state of ecstasy. He spoke with great reverence when he mentioned 'Master Soul' White Eagle. 'Guides say, "He has much authority,"' said Peter. As an aside he said, 'We must be careful what we say, because they don't welcome praise. Our guides say that they stand aside for Master Soul White Eagle when he comes.'

Over the next two years I spoke to Peter many times on the telephone and had several long discussions with him at his home. Peter would answer any question; he would often pause briefly while he found suitable words for the mental prompts that he told me he received.

We rarely chatted about personal matters. Peter accepted that his role was to be available to pass on information. Unlike Joy, who was thrilled with being able to teach, and was pleased when I could spend some social time with her, Peter was friendly and obliging but more impersonal. He was not helping me for any personal glory or for any social reason. He told me that I did not have to bring any biscuits or anything else when I had my meetings with him — just bring myself. His talks were about what choices and opportunities I had if I was serious about wanting to lead a genuine spiritual life, and how it was best for me to proceed.

'You *are* an initiate,' he told me after I had conversed with him for several months. 'Some things like numerology and seeing auras are interesting, but they are not really important on a spiritual level.

'Sai Baba is offering to be your guru,' he told me one day. 'He is helping you a limited amount already; you are truly fortunate.'

Peter was obviously a very devotional person. He said that he felt very humble because he felt a great love from God. He told me that the feeling was so joyous that he had difficulty describing it.

Involuntary astral travel

It had become a habit for me to meditate at 11 am every day using the method Joy had taught me. As usual I had lain down on my bed. Sitting straight-backed was difficult for me because my faulty back and hips prevented it. I stereteched out, relaxed, and closed my eyes and took a few deep, steady breaths. I had learned from experience that this should start the process of meditation that had become normal for me as soon as I could relax and slow down my busy mind. Everything became hazy and soon I was surprised when I looked at my watch to find that half an hour had passed. Had I been half asleep?

I closed my eyes again. Almost immediately I began to 'see' pale yellow rings that looked like smoke rings passing around me from behind. As they had always done in the past, they encircled my head before they slowly wafted past me one at a time at about four second intervals, then they continued onwards until they faded away. When this had happened at the onset of some meditations in the past, I had always become unaware of anything exterior for up to an hour.

Then the unexpected happened. Suddenly, I felt a physical jolt and an invisible force pinned my arms to my side and forced my body and legs to straighten and stiffen immediately. I was helpless as I was being sent rocketing feet first at an incredible speed. My head had been drawn back and forced to twist to the right against the pillow, and I was whooshing somewhere so fast that it was almost impossible to breathe or think. It was a frightening feeling. I was struggling to breathe and the muscles in my chest seemed paralysed. I was vaguely aware of a loud, continuous slurping sound very close by. It took a tremendous effort to focus my attention on what was causing the weird noise. It was me involuntarily sucking in air — my lungs felt as if they had been forced towards my mouth and I was struggling to breathe. It was as if a powerful elastic bungee had yanked me from my bed. But I knew that I must still be bodily present in my room, so I was confused. I stopped redirecting my focus and submitted to the necessity of trying to cope with my 'real' situation but I understood that I must still be lying on my bed. With a tremendous effort, I managed to open my eyes. I saw my 'real' surroundings, my bedroom, as if through frosted spectacles. Realising that I might break the psychic connection, I stopped resisting and my eyelids clamped tightly shut again. I wanted to continue with this experience. My fear faded: I was still feeling anxious, but I was now sure this must be part of my spiritual experience. My throat now felt bone dry as I zoomed on, disorientated. It reminded me of my youth when I was on a galloping horse with no saddle, barely able to control it. Time seemed irrelevant now.

I was astonished to find myself unexpectedly floating weightless and immobile and feeling released from any constriction, although I had not sensed myself slowing down. I could 'see' now with perfect clarity. Surrounding me was a blue sky dotted with dozens of silver specks, like stars. I was aware that what I was seeing had the appearance of a painting. There was not any sense of up or down, no gravity, 'Just like Aladdin on his flying carpet,' I thought later. I had to stir my numb mind to think. Why had this happened?

Not wanting to waste this experience, I tried to feel appreciative and to fully comprehend my situation, because it might not last long. I was not giving any thought now to whether I was breathing or was in my body. This was a place where it seemed that neither time nor gravity had any reason or influence. I would have preferred to be without any thoughts and just enjoy the peace, but was I here to learn something?

A short time passed before I was suddenly gripped firmly again. It felt as if I was being constrained by a rocket-propelled straitjacket, because immediately I was zooming along again in my own typhoon, sightless, at what felt like a reckless speed. There was a weird feeling in my stomach and heart area, and I was gasping for air again as I shuddered along.

Suddenly I panicked, because I felt as if I had been dropped, so I frantically threw my arms out wide to try to save myself. To my amazement I was back on the bed; the innersprung mattress had caused me to bounce as I 'landed'. All pressure on my body had ceased but I felt shaken up and exhausted. I had opened my eyes in alarm, frightened by the apparent fall. My throat was parched, and I desperately needed a drink to help me recover my strength and my wits, so I sipped some water from a glass that I had placed beside the bed. I was feeling bewildered and exhausted.

The telephone jangled, startling me. I struggled to my feet and staggered to the landline phone. 'Hello,' I managed to croak, trying to speak in my usual voice.

It was Joy. 'How are you, David?' she asked.

I wondered if that was a trick question. Did she already know what had happened to me? This was the first time that she had ever rung me.

'I just had an interesting experience,' I said, purposely understating what had happened. I wondered how anybody could believe what I had to say, but then I felt certain that Joy would believe my story.

'Why, what happened?' she asked. It seemed that she did not know — or was she teasing me? I explained what had happened.

Joy responded without hesitation: 'What did you think about that?' She did not seem surprised, but I knew that she would be excited for me. She had recently told me about some of her own spiritual-psychic experiences. I told her I was emotionally overwhelmed.

'Were you frightened?' Joy asked.

'At first I was shocked, but you had said, "How can any harm come to you if you are a good person, if you have prayed for protection, and if you are confident that you are safe?"'

What I had experienced was a dimension commonly called the astral in the West, but a state that could be described as close to earth. Fifteen years later I was to learn that I had briefly experienced a semi-material state, or dimension, described in Buddhist and Hindu philosophy as a region of desire.

Troublesome spirit beings (haunted)

Rebecca was an attractive 34-year-old woman — a professional singer who had performed at Sky City. She was a natural psychic — who occasionally attended one of the spiritualist churches that I regularly volunteered at. I had first met her when she had come to consult me when I had a brief spell as a professional tarot card reader. One day I was surprised when she came knocking at my door accompanied by Kate, a Maori friend about her age that I had read cards for about two years earlier. I had not known that the two women knew each other.

'Would you please come to my house?' asked Rebecca, sounding hopeful. 'Kate says that she needs a man present to provide a male energy. We have unfriendly spirits in my house, and they are scaring my children and me. Kate is going to do a traditional Maori cleansing.'

That sounded like it would be interesting and exciting. I asked her for the address and told her I would be along soon. I decided to ask for advice from Peter before I left home. Joy had mentioned that she had been with Peter when he had been called to clear spirits from a house. She said that Peter had chanted in a foreign language, which I guessed was probably a Sanskrit mantra, because he told me he studied Indian philosophy.

'Oh yes! That will be okay,' he said when I rang him. 'You will be quite safe. Before you go, pray to Master Sai Baba for protection and you will not have to worry. Just do what the Maori healer wants; follow her lead. Before you enter the house, pray again. You can use the same prayer that you usually use, but you must be in a raised condition like you are when you are doing spiritual healing. Let me know what happened when you get home.'

Before I performed spiritual healing on anyone, I always focused on being mentally calm. I knew that the most important attitude for me to adopt was to have sincere intentions, so the words of any prayer had to be sincerely meant.

This was the prayer that Joy had taught me:

May the light of God surround me,

May the love of God enfold me,

May the power of God protect me,

And may the presence of God be with me,

For in truth, we are one, and all will be well.

So be it,

Amen.

I recited the prayer and then I drove to Rebecca's house where I repeated the prayer. Kate met me outside the house and handed me some sliced bread. 'Bury some at each corner of the property, please,' she said. There was no implement available to dig the soil with, so she said, 'Just place the bread on the ground.' Rebecca and her two pre-teen daughters were outside looking very subdued. Kate held a small bowl of water: 'It has been blessed,' she said, and we all entered the house. She instructed everyone to follow behind her. Her cheeks were flushed as she started chanting a karakia, an incantation in the Maori language, as she flicked the water over clumps of hair that Rebecca said had been put around the living room by her ex-boyfriend. From brief comments that were made, I understood that Rebecca considered that her ex-boyfriend had been involved in unconventional psychic studies and practices.

She worried that he had tried to put a curse on her. Rebecca and her two children and I followed close behind Kate as she moved forward. I reached out my hand — I wanted to find out if I could feel any psychic energy, but I could not. Before we reached the next room, Rebecca suddenly let out a cry of relief: 'They've gone!' Kate explained that the spirits of tribal people had returned to where they had lived on the land that Rebecca's home stood on. Now they had left to go to the light.

Later I rang Peter and told him what had happened and that everything had gone well. He enquired about the method Kate had used. He told me: 'There are many methods of achieving the necessary result, which was to assist the spirits to continue on to where they were supposed to be, and not keep causing problems for the present occupants of the land. The main thing was that it worked,' he said.

'I didn't see or feel anything,' I said.

'You aren't psychic, and you do not have to be because you are a channel,' said Peter matter-of-factly.

Not psychic? That statement confirmed what Mark had told me: I am able, or had the potential to be able, to channel — but what would I channel? Words, or some sort of energy? It had not occurred to me to include spiritual healing, psychometry, dowsing and counselling as examples of channelling. Was praying channelling?

Chapter 9
More church experiences

Joy's advice

Joy served as a regular spiritual healer at the spiritualist churches; she told me that she had been attending their services for many years. She talked to me as if I had every right to know all about her own personal spiritual growth and her interesting experiences. She told me that on one of her meditations she had heard some enthralling music getting gradually louder. 'It sounded like a Russian men's choir. Then I remembered that there had been a tragic accident in Russian waters — a submarine had sunk, and the crew could not be rescued. I asked, "There are so many souls — how will I cope?" I was told to form them into rows. I directed the rows into a church that appeared. Light streamed through multicoloured stained-glass windows high up on a wall, and so I directed the men to march into the light in tidy columns, as they sung with gusto. Row by row they were absorbed into the light until the last ones had disappeared.'

One day Joy paid a visit to see me at home. Why had she come? She had never called to see me before. We briefly chatted over afternoon tea.

'Choose a master,' she said suddenly, without having previously indicated that she was going to say anything of importance.

'Sai Baba,' I answered after a brief pause.

Surprised as I was at this sudden change of subject, I understood that it must not have been Joy's idea to suddenly blurt those words out; she must have had an inner prompting. I had heard that a Sai Baba devotee was expected to produce results from the spiritual assistance given by him. White Eagle was a teacher: I would possibly have been able to pass on messages 'from the spirit' if I had chosen White Eagle, but maybe he will still be working through me and I will not be aware of it. He had said that he could 'use me very well'. Francie Williams had told her students that they should choose a *compatible* master, and Peter had stated that it was important to focus on our chosen master only, and so had Francie.

When I attended several spiritualist churches within travelling distance of home I was often being told by platform speakers and psychics that I was a healer, and that I should be teaching. I knew that I had to be confident about my innate ability to be a healer; it would be withholding my service if I doubted myself. I always said an appropriate prayer in my head before I commenced any healing. One of the women that I was giving healing to surprised me when she told me that she saw a winged white horse.

Since my time as a student at the parapsychology school, I had been following Francie's advice and kept a diary. The purpose was to keep myself in a positive frame of mind since I had become certain that I was gradually ascending a spiritual ladder. Because I had had a few incredible experiences and they might stop at any time, I wanted to be able to look back at the diary entries to keep confident that I was on the right track to progress spiritually. I had already had some extraordinary experiences and I suppose I was not expecting the encouraging messages or advice to continue for ever. Entries in my diaries were recording messages from mediums who were visiting platform speakers, and from psychics in the congregation who gave me information. I recorded any teaching or information from White Eagle or from my friends. Several times, I was told that I studied books too much and I did not need any instruction by anyone, because I would be taught from within; I should get out and about with people more often.

Soon after I had become a regular at several spiritualist churches, I decided to buy a tape recorder and record the platform speakers' addresses to the congregations, with the speakers' permission. I listened to the tapes again later at home to see how much detail the medium on the platform had given. I suppose I was attempting to make a thorough survey to investigate how much valid information the mediums provided, and I would also have a record of what I had experienced in case I would ever manage to write a book.

I was a volunteer as one of the regular healers at two of the churches. Some of the other healers would pass on intuitive messages about the health of their 'patient' or about something personal, but I rarely had any intuitional information to pass on.

Open circles and messages from mediums

A common activity of mediums is to have meetings, or 'circles', at a private home or in a hired room. There are '*open*' circles for anyone curious about learning whether they can enhance their own psychic abilities or wishing to gain an understanding of how to interpret what they see or hear intuitively. The circles provided an opportunity to discover developing mediums. Usually, the majority of those present are psychic, and occasionally someone may have an extra quality of seership, capable of giving remarkable predictions. Exceptionally psychic participants may be invited to move to a '*closed*' circle to receive more detailed training from an experienced medium. They may become a platform medium after they have shown they are capable and responsible. Some people are professional mediums in their private lives, working for a fee to support themselves and their family. Joy told me that in the United Kingdom there was strict control over the mediums' training, and there was a system of certification of mediums.

Mediums are often represented in movies in a way that is probably what used to happen over a hundred years ago, when some mediums had those attending sitting in circles in darkened rooms holding hands and hoping for a message from a 'dear departed' friend or relative. There had also been some famous frauds, but in modern times there is good lighting and a friendly, relaxed atmosphere. Some mediums say that they hear many voices asking to be chosen so that their message can be passed on. According to Joy, the medium's guide should be the one who chooses who is going to 'come through' and then there is no confusion.

I attended one open circle dozens of times. A brief introductory prayer of protection was always said to ask that only positive influences be present. A short meditation followed, after which the leader asked what, if anything, had been seen, felt, or heard by the participants during the meditation.

I was originally concerned that the organisers of the circles might be attempting to force psychic growth, and I did not want to attend because I did not believe that I was psychic or could become so. I had decided that to proceed with attempts to fast-track any psychic or spiritual gifts, without successful efforts to improve one's character first, seemed unwise. It could be likened to a learner driver being in control of a racing car. There was little mention in the spiritualist churches that I attended about encouraging improvement in what I considered to be personal characteristics. Some of the mediums' messages did occasionally contain advice that was intended to diplomatically inform some of the listeners that their negative attitudes should be corrected. Perhaps some of them were concentrating only on wanting to be better psychics. *Spiritual* understanding and advancement should be achieved if there was an effort by each individual person to appreciate that they are themselves always a work in progress. I had become aware that self-discipline, together with any development of psychic or spiritual capabilities, was essential to be enabled to develop safely. I was aiming to know the Truth, i.e., to intuitively be able to access the Truth — Wisdom — from the dimension where it is in its own realm. Over the next 20 years I would gradually gain more assurance that I was connected to this dimension when impediments were removed.

I decided to regularly attend an open circle after I was unexpectedly elected the vice president of one of the churches after I had been a member for five years. Mediums or clairvoyants were always needed to give demonstrations, and the untrained mediums and psychics required advice from those who were more experienced. For example: what might it mean if the psychic sees a book in their inner vision? Does it mean that the person is a student, or needs to study, or should read more or write a book? Perhaps they are reading too much.

The key to the interpretation of symbolic visions experienced while meditating — or perhaps even unexpected experiences that can happen without warning even when not consciously meditating — needs to be discovered. Understanding the meaning of spiritual symbology is essential if it is to be of practical use, and some dreams may be implying an important event. In the years ahead I was to have regular visions and could not always interpret what was being inferred.

Peter told me that the energy source for spiritual healing and the exact shade of healing colour and quantity, and the method of delivery, are all decided on at a higher dimension; this has also been described in some White Eagle books. It comes as required and permitted according to the requirements *and karma* of the person receiving the healing. The healer has no need to be aware of *exactly* what is happening. We do not really decide what to do — God does, according to Peter; everything is included within the Universal Essence of Nature. Because the terminology used for the doer by White Eagle is Great White Spirit, this implies that there is an impersonal doer. This is the Buddhist view.

A medium at a distant church that I visited had asked for permission to come to me. 'Your mother is here. She shows me a bony hand. She says that she was all skin and bones when she got older. She says that you have been using your tarot cards and dowsing, but you do not need to. You have been through all that. It is time to go inside to your heart centre; use your intuition.' It was now the year 2000.

I often think that some of these well-meant messages that gave me encouragement also gave me an apparently unsolvable problem. How can I make a spiritual breakthrough and achieve the things that I am being told I can do? How would I know if Sai Baba was assisting me, or White Eagle? I believe that I can only do my best to concentrate my thoughts and efforts and believe that my aspirations are registered in an appropriate dimension — then I would get what I deserved. At Marie's home I had been told to not be concerned about my spiritual progress.

It was several years before I realised that any spiritual advancement is not always obvious, and patience, determination and willpower is part of the course of discipline. I should not make being aware of progress one of my aims. I felt confident that the persistent yearning in my heart would lead me to where I was supposed to be, spiritually, psychically, and physically. After my introduction to tarot cards and numerology, I was determined to prove the validity of a spiritual universe, even if it is only proven to myself. However, I had no idea what incredible results my persistence was going to bring. I always kept a record of every significant experience because I wanted to eventually share the experiences that I was having; that there are dimensions other than what most people are aware of. There had to be a cosmic management system that may be beyond any human being's understanding. Religious theories will not always be correct and should never have been set in concrete. They surely have strayed away from the simple truths that the original teachers were attempting to open the listeners' hearts and minds to. Ultimately, I believe that we do not choose *exactly* what to do. I am now certain that what is *needed* will be provided according to universal laws already established.

I kept receiving a steady flow of messages from the mediums and clairvoyants at the spiritualist churches. I will give only a few examples because I have about 200 diary entries. I lost two diaries covering two important years and recorded many speakers at spiritualist churches, with their permission, mostly between 1997 and 2004, when I was transferred to work in Auckland.

'There's an old man playing an accordion — an old-fashioned one with buttons: "We have smoothed the way," he says.' I remembered that my grandfather had a button accordion that he played once or twice when I was about nine years old. It must have been his entertainment when he was younger before the radio stations were established. This was a message that I had received at a spiritualist church soon after I began to attend. Then: 'Don't worry about people you can't help.' I considered this message to be important.

I had had a vivid dream one night soon after I started practising meditating: I picked up some spectacles, but when I was about to put them on it appeared that they were not mine because they had gold frames. I heard a voice say, 'You have new eyes now. You will see things differently.'

I had been feeling frustrated with my apparently slow spiritual progress when I had another dream. Several unseen people gave me hugs and were lovingly touching and squeezing me. An enthusiastic woman radiating joy approached and kissed me, then walked away, leaving me feeling loved and supported. It was perhaps a trivial event, but this dream gave me another boost of confidence. At that time, I had not had any apparent result from meditating except that my thighs felt as if they were being frozen. It was comforting to remember that my frightening childhood nightmares about being unable to escape a pursuer stopped after I had a dream that I was Superman when I was 14 years old. In hindsight, had this been my first symbolic spiritual message?

One medium at a church told me that she had a doctor with her who had attended to me when I was a young boy. He apologised to me for being rough when he examined my broken arm. I had a vague memory of seeing a doctor when I was about seven years old. 'He is saying that you are ready to be a channel.' While starting to write this book — 15 years after receiving the message — an older sister of mine confirmed that I had broken a bone in my arm and was taken to be examined by a doctor.

On one occasion a clairvoyant on the platform gave me a dramatic and thought-provoking message: 'I knew that I had a message for you as soon as I came in the door and saw you. You are a healer, aren't you? You are going to have an amazing surge of energy. You will know when it starts. Just go along with whatever happens. Tidy up your books because you are going to be busy!' Two years later I would be in India, and that prediction about energy was to sensationally come true. On my return to New Zealand, I would start a new career.

After the service, I went to speak with the clairvoyant.

'You don't need the books,' she said. 'You will have the knowledge within.' This woman had astounded me several times in the past with her astonishing clairvoyance. Some platform speakers were not so much mediums as seers — future tellers.

During conversations with Peter, he told me: 'You don't have much karma. You have worked through materialism in previous lives. You will know all — you do not need books. You are here to ascend so you don't need to be instructed by anyone.' Similar messages had been relayed to me several times in the past. Ascending probably meant to rise to another level of consciousness. I hope to clarify for readers what I have experienced, and to give them hope that eventually, there can be noticeable spiritual progress in their own life.

Chapter 10
Spiritual masters

Predictions

Joy seemed vague about her reasons for not wanting to accompany me to Marie's for a visit when we were both invited again, so I went by myself. White Eagle spoke to me, but I do not have a record of what he told me. Marie thanked me for my warning months ago about her needing to rest to avoid a heart problem. I had been having doubts that my interpretation of the cards for her was accurate.

'Everything that you told me has happened. First, I had angina. I cut down my work and made sure to have a rest during the day.' I think she told me this to give me confidence that I should tell people for whom I read tarot cards the truth as I interpreted it.

When I got home, I rang Peter. Sai Baba was continuing to offer to be my guru, he said. 'You are extremely fortunate. He is helping you a limited amount already; at these times Master

Soul White Eagle stands aside. Ask Sai Baba to teach and guide you — use his name.'

What is a guru? Wikipedia says: 'Sanskrit: teacher, master. Oral tradition: *experiential wisdom transmitted* from teacher to student. One who dispels the darkness of ignorance.'

I visited Nancy, the friend of Joy, Peter, and Marie who I have mentioned previously. She was the mother of two teenage children.

'Is he one of us?' Nancy had enquired when I was first being introduced by Marie.

'Yes, he is,' had been Marie's reply.

Nancy had informed me: 'White Eagle is the head of the White Brotherhood. He's a teacher — Jesus and Sai Baba are healers.' She told me that she asks Sai Baba to solve any problem, even trivial ones, because he had invited her to do that, she said. She commented that tarot and numerology readings that I had done for two of her friends had pleased them. When I was leaving her home after visiting her on one occasion, she was accompanying me to the door when she suddenly turned and went back inside. Seconds later she came back and handed me a large piece of amethyst crystal — 'I was told to give this to you.' I had become used to unexpected things happening by then. Later I read that amethyst emanates vibrations that help to promote clear thinking, peace, and psychic abilities.

Phyllis Tantrum (her real name) was an elderly woman for whom many people had enormous respect because of her remarkable demonstrations of mediumship and clairvoyance. She had initiated several spiritualist churches. I had never met her, but I had listened to her when she had been featured regularly on a radio programme, and I was given a message from her once when she was a visiting medium on the platform. On that occasion she had told me that I was not to worry about my young son's future because he was going to be all right — he would have a good job. Fifteen years later he had become the owner of a successful precision engineering factory.

Months later, in the year 2000, Phyllis was one of the mediums giving readings at a fundraising evening for a spiritualist church when I joined a group of people sitting around her. Phyllis spent a long time with me. I tape-recorded Phyllis talking to me.

'You need to sit in the shade,' Phyllis told me. 'Evelyn is here.' My mother's name was Evelyn. 'She wiped your head. Did you have hepatitis?' I had been ill once as a child and had been delirious. '"You're a better colour now!" she says. Your grandmother gives you a four-leaf clover. Wear it next to your heart. Your flat is too small — move out. There is so much more for you to look forward to. Do you pray? Yes — you do. It is all very well to be spiritual, but you have to be in this world. There is an interesting time to come over the next two years, when 2002 ends. Uncle Jack [my father's deceased younger brother?] says to lay the foundation for a new path. You are a lovely healer — there is much more to look forward to. You have to face the world.' I was still studying my books daily and trying to keep positive because I was unemployed. 'You have a lot of encouragement from spirit. An Irish lady loves the way you think. She used to read the Bible.' My mother's mother was Irish and Catholic, and so was her grandmother. 'The New Year will bring its rewards. There is a wonderful year coming up. The house where you lived when you were born has gone.' Years later I discovered that the house where my family used to live had been demolished. I had not known that my father had previously owned a house before he bought a farm. 'Your new house will have a tap broken. It is blocked up. The toilet system has problems, and the house is overgrown. There will be doves there — you're going to love it!' As I was writing these words that Phyllis had spoken 20 years ago, gardeners had finished taking away five truckloads of the overgrown garden that had been advancing nearer to my back door, and the building had recently been repainted and repaired. When I sat in my lounge, I could see pigeons foraging for food, including a native kereru from a window overlooking a lawn. New plumbing had to be fitted under the kitchen sink because the water stopped flowing, and the bath drain had to be unblocked. A pipe under the hot water cylinder began to leak, and water seeped through the front wall during wet weather. A plumber had to replace the shower plumbing. Every fault has been rectified since I moved in. Phyllis had been correct.

At this time, I did not know that some of the messages indicated that I should prepare for a complete career change, but it would be 16 years before I lived in a property like the one that Phyllis described.

Marie rang me at home once, because she had had a vision and wanted to tell me urgently. She said to ask Nancy's guide what it meant because there was not time for her to explain then because her husband was home and did not approve of her spiritual interests. She had secluded herself to make this hasty phone call.

'You were sitting in a high-backed chair,' said Marie. 'On your head was a golden crown. In your hand was a golden sceptre. The cloak on your shoulders was a pale mauve silk.'

'You have been given more responsibility,' was Nancy's immediate response when I rang her. 'You have passed an initiation. You have your foot on the bottom of a new ladder.' Joy and Peter both confirmed this interpretation when I told them about it later.

White Eagle has been quoted as saying that there are both major and minor initiations in life. Many minor ones pass unnoticed; they occur when there is some turmoil in our lives. Perhaps I had passed certain tests, or maybe it could be said that I had met the standards necessary. However, an initiate would be fully aware of any major initiations, but I had not been aware of any such process. Everyone must eventually pass all challenges in their lives. Taking appropriate ethical actions when confronted with difficulties was imperative.

Soon afterwards, Peter told me, 'You have been through primary school, high school, and university, and now you're doing your doctorate. You are commencing knowledge of earth mastership.'

Now, as I write these words, I am reading various notes that I made at the time, and I read that White Eagle said that earth mastership relates to ceasing yearning and not being tempted by material things — use them, but wisely. Do not lust after them in a grasping way.

Several years earlier I had had an unusual dream — a structure on my right tumbled slowly through space towards my left; it was made up of many thin rods like a folding clothes rack or a

Ferris wheel without the seats, but more spaced out. The rods were various pastel colours: red, green, yellow, blue, and lilac. I had an impression that it was an Indian-inspired structure because of the shades of colour. I did not know then that Indian spiritual influences on my life were soon going to increase.

At a spiritualist church I got a message that seemed to come from my stepmother. 'I have a mother here,' said the medium. 'She was plump but lost weight in later years. She did not like swearing. She was slightly built and short. She died quite suddenly. She says, "Do not worry about a move coming up because everything will be okay. You have been in a stagnant patch in your life lately but do not be surprised if you go off on a tangent. You might have to do some things differently to what you expected. Your dad did not go grey much or lose all his hair like you. He was a nice man. The big black dog is here too, and they all love you. Don't worry about George [my stepfather, my mother's second husband]. You always tried to be nice to him when visiting him. He has not been well lately and is getting prepared. He will be fine. He is aware."' Aware of what? I wondered. He was already 81 years old, so that could mean that he knows that his life in a body is nearly finished. It was interesting that my stepmother had never met George.

'Who knows a George?' another medium asked at a church service. Three people raised their hands — I was one of them.

'It's for you there,' she said, pointing to me. 'It's appreciated by spirit that you have always tried to get along with George.' My stepfather loved his daily beers after work. He had jokingly complained when I once bought low-alcohol beer for him because he was soon going to be driving a long distance. 'Why?'

he wanted to know. 'Why drink beer if you don't want to get drunk?' A few months later he did die, and I received an unexpected legacy from him that had first been predicted about 35 years previously. My mother had died 15 years before him.

Sketch of a master

On a visit to Marie, she handed me some money and told me to go immediately to keep an appointment she had made for me to be sketched at a local shop, where a visiting intuitive artist was working. The artist was a handsome woman about 30 years old. She told me that as she looked at me and started to sketch in pastels, she became aware of what colours she should use. The sketch showed a native American man about 50 years old, wearing a full-feathered headdress standing tall behind me with his left arm around me. His right hand was open with the fingers extended, palm down, close to the top of my head. I knew that it must be White Eagle, because Marie had previously given me a picture of another intuitive artist's impression of him, and this likeness was similar. Marie was pleased with the sketch when I showed it to her later.

Three weeks later I moved out of my friend's house. The messages that I had been given about changes to my circumstances were partly confirmed.

Chapter 11
Troublesome spirits again

REBECCA PHONED ME AND TOLD ME THAT SHE WAS being threatened by a spirit being again. Would I come back to her home? Her Maori healer friend Kate had recently died, so she could not be called upon to help. Rebecca agreed with my suggestion to ask Peter for advice, and when I did, Peter surprised me by offering to meet us at Rebecca's home on the following Saturday.

'A man is threatening me. He wants to have sex with me,' said Rebecca as soon as I arrived on Saturday.

'How could he be back again?' I asked, puzzled. 'You said he had gone.' Rebecca's two girls were listening, looking anxious.

'It's a different man,' said Rebecca sheepishly.

That surprised me. 'How could this happen? You said you weren't going to allow yourself to encourage any spirit beings trying to communicate with you.'

Rebecca looked embarrassed. 'It was boring not having any spirit communication — I'm so used to it. It is not so lonely then. At first a man was very friendly but eventually he started threatening me. He told me that he would harm me if I didn't agree to his demands.' Her children were paying close attention to our conversation.

'Did you girls see him too?' I asked. They both nodded.

Peter arrived and was introduced to the family. He sat calmly with the children and assured them that everything would soon be back to normal. 'Sometimes spirit beings may not be aware that they have died and passed to the spirit world. We must help them because they haven't completely gone to where they are supposed to go.'

I sat down with the children while Peter was talking to Rebecca, because they looked very worried. 'What did you see?' I asked them. One of the girls made a small diagram on paper with the coloured pencils that I had brought. She drew a simple multicoloured star-like pattern — not a human figure — so I guessed that she must have seen psychic energy as colour. As usual, I wanted to get whatever evidence I could.

'It's no good coming here to try to chase him away,' said Peter. 'He'd probably come back later anyway; he'd just jump out the window if he were worried about us. We must help him with love, so before I left home, I prayed to Sai Baba for protection, and immediately I saw a pink ribbon of love linking me to him. On the way here I had the intention of helping the spirit being with love — that is why he is not frightened of me. We must all have the intention of assisting him to go where he is supposed to go.' Usually a gentler method than Francie had used in Auckland.

'Where is he supposed to go?' asked one of the children. 'What if he doesn't want to go?' asked the other girl.

'First, he's offered a chance to move on in the spirit world voluntarily,' said Peter. 'Then if he won't go — let us say he will be taken away to a place where he can't do any harm. He can behave however he likes — he cannot cause any trouble, but sooner or later he will have to decide to go to the light and face up to his past actions. Sometimes spirit beings are afraid of going to the light, but that is where they are supposed to go. Sometimes they stay where they are and do not move on because they have not realised that they are in the spirit world. They are not aware that they are physically dead.'

Peter turned to me: 'Just follow me when I walk around the house. I will hold out my hand and walk around every room — you could do the same. There will be energy coming from your hand just like when you do spiritual healing. Put your hand in every corner and cupboard, and if there is nothing there, we will have to go to any outside buildings. The spirit beings hide in them sometimes.'

'I don't think that I'll see anything,' I said truthfully.

'You don't need to, just do what I do,' Peter replied.

We started off in the room that we were in, and so I extended my hand into a cupboard but felt nothing. Peter was silently moving ahead of me and went into the next room; Rebecca and the children were behind me.

'He's gone,' Rebecca said abruptly, which broke the silence. We had hardly started! It seemed a repeat of the last time when Rebecca's spirits had decided to go voluntarily.

'Yes, he's gone,' agreed Peter. The children looked relieved.

I wondered why Rebecca seemed to have had regular visits from annoying and sometimes malicious spirit beings. It was becoming obvious to me that she must be a natural medium. She was quite headstrong and did not like to be restricted in her thinking and actions. She would have to want to be free from unrestricted interference from spirits.

Some people visualise a protective circle of light around them. In the past I had tried that after Dean, the teacher at Francie's parapsychology school, had mentioned that he did it while taking his morning shower, so that he would be safe during the day. I was pleasantly surprised when that method worked for me to limit my stress levels when I was busy working during that period. The main thing would be to do whatever is sincerely intended.

Joy told me she had been with Peter on another occasion when he had chanted in a foreign language as she followed him around. Peter told me that he mentally heard chanting when he was doing his ritual cleansing.

Joy had explained to me that some people may hear a spirit voice wanting to communicate with them. Joy's advice was to ask, 'Can you stand in the light?' The spirit cannot lie in response to that challenge. 'They may feel frightened to move on from where they found themselves after passing over, so that is why they stay in a lower vibration that is close to the earth vibration, or they may possibly have a strong desire to remain in a body on earth so they can keep experiencing earth's sensations.'

Peter had said, 'It is not taken for granted that you want protection unless you ask for it, but when you ask it is instantly given.' He advised me to always say a protective prayer.

I feel I should add extra information to give the reader more details about 'life' after 'death' of the body. Many years have passed since the events described above happened and I have learned and experienced much since. I am recalling the past as I saw it at the time. Everyone has a lifespan that is due to them. If they should die by accident, murder, war, or illness, prematurely, they usually will not pass from the spiritual atmosphere that they find themselves in until the expiration of the lifespan that they should have had is completed. If they were a person that was very materialistic, especially if they were exceedingly hedonistic, they probably would strongly desire to continue with their previous lifestyle. Such people may not realise that they are, in fact, dead. Some of these spirits may want to communicate with living people and continue experiencing the sensations that they had enjoyed when in a body. When their lifespan is eventually over, they will naturally move on to where they should have gone if they had died at the expiration of their expected lifespan. The truly spiritual aspects of their earthly life, including all their happy memories, will be retained, and transferred to what most Westerners would call heaven — and some Buddhist sects have named The Pure Land — after the negative and irrelevant aspects of their life have been dissipated. This intermediate period may be delayed for some souls while their past actions and thoughts are sifted by natural processes but will conclude after being evaluated. Children who die during the first seven years of their life will return promptly and be reborn; they would not have to go through any confusing state first, wondering what had happened to them. Buddhists believe that this heaven stage is a temporary pause before being born into another body, bearing the spiritual qualities that had already been established, but with a fresh set of personal attributes.

Chapter 12
Sathya Sai Baba

I sing Indian hymns, called bhajans

I HAD READ THE BOOK THAT MARIE HAD GIVEN ME — *Sai Baba: Man of Miracles* by Howard Murphet. I was astounded that in these modern times such a person as Sathya Sai Baba existed. However, according to the author, he must be living proof of what I had always assumed — that surely there must be spiritual masters alive on the earth at any stage of history. Sai Baba could speak in detail about spiritual matters of any religion without resorting to written material. What was fascinating was that he repeatedly told listeners that all people are embodiments of love.

Howard Murphet had been president of the Theosophical Society of Australia and had written several thought-provoking philosophical books. He and his wife Iris had toured India in the 1960s; they had visited various ashrams to try to locate any genuine spiritual masters, but the famous founders of the established ashrams they called at were all dead and their followers carried on as best as they could. Eventually, the Murphets were taken to see Sathya Sai Baba. Howard was certain he had found a genuine guru, a 'dispeller of darkness'. Sai Baba taught that every person is a spark of divinity; every person is potentially God. God is the source of every person's being and everyone must eventually realise that. Sai Baba said that he knows that he is God, but most other people are not aware that their own true self is also God.

Thousands of people travelled to see Sai Baba at his ashram in an isolated desert village in India. They recognised him as a guru — a genuine spiritual master. A master has been described as one who is adept at nature, working in harmony with evolutionary forces.

Sai Baba had been famous since he was a child. He produced gifts for devotees from 'nowhere'. On some occasions, he waved his hand in a circular motion with his palm facing down and an ash-like powder that Indians call vibhuti fell into devotees' extended hands. Howard witnessed these events many times. With his wife Iris he spent months in Sai Baba's company before he became famous internationally. They often travelled with him when he visited poor villages in his region, and they stayed in the same house as Sai Baba on the ashram. Iris often ironed Sai Baba's clothes and she noted that there were no hidden pockets. Sai Baba lived very simply and ate sparingly, just enough to sustain good health.

The ashram was run by a trust. Over the years since Howard had first visited, free schools, and the free Super Specialty Hospital — that I had seen in the earlier video presentation — and accommodation for hundreds of visiting devotees had been built. Similar facilities extended to some other parts of

India; the trust had responsibility for billions of dollars' worth of assets.

I was curious to know what the local Sathya Sai Baba branch did. I had been told that the devotees always meet on a Thursday evening — the night Indians traditionally honour their own guru. I had read that hundreds of Sathya Sai Baba branches are spread throughout the world.

I was fascinated by what I discovered when I participated in the meetings. The Sai Baba organisation was non-denominational. There were chants which everyone seemed to know, and hymns — called bhajans — were sung. Most of the bhajans were in the Sanskrit language, a language used in India in ancient times. Singing in Sanskrit allowed for some commonality of the devotees' different dialects and languages in India and around the world, but there were some bhajans with English words, and sometimes a Maori-language bhajan would be sung.

I started to go to a Sai Baba bhajan practice in a private home regularly. I was surprised and nervous because my intention was to be there in support of the competent singers, but I was asked to lead a bhajan, that is, I had to sing solo, after which the words would be repeated by the other members. I had never sung in my life, but I felt that I could not refuse to try, because the other singers were so enthusiastic. During regular meetings the singing was accompanied by musicians, and as the drums beat out their rhythms and I grew familiar with them coordinating with my singing I was raised to a blissful emotional level. After a few weeks I had mastered the art of taking a breath at an appropriate time while singing my solo lines, instead of running out of puff. I know that I was not a good singer, but I was enthusiastic.

I had purchased a book containing the words of the bhajans, and a cassette of some popular bhajans was given to me. I found myself playing the cassette at home so many times that I learned the Sanskrit words by heart because I felt overjoyed to hear the music. Soon I was often leading the singing of a bhajan on Thursday nights when most of the members were present. I recalled a relevant Indian story that I had read: a master took a student to a river and held his head underwater so long that when the student was released, he was gasping for air. The master told him that he should long for God as much as he longed for air. That is the way that I was feeling, but my idea of what God could be was very vague and was eventually to change.

At this stage of my life the singing in the churches and the singing with the Sai Baba devotees had a harmonising effect, helping to bring unity and peace to the assemblies. I assumed that the vibrations were raised, and so promoted the receptiveness of the participants to spiritual influences. The literal meaning of the songs was not as important as the spiritual effect on the participants.

Devotees regarded Sai Baba as an avatar, an incarnation of God, and an avatar that they were fortunate to be able to personally visit. Previous avatars in Indian history were Rama and Krishna — and Jesus, the Buddha, and Shirdi Sai Baba are regarded as avatars by some Indians.

The 'Spiritual Day', 2000

I had been going to the various events advertised as a Spiritual Day, Psychic Fair or similar; whenever I saw one advertised, I would attend. I was following my strong inner urge to make more spiritual discoveries and possibly have some sort of breakthrough of a spiritual nature. Ever since I started to learn about the psychic/spiritual world, I felt the need to seek out people who had some personal awareness and understanding of these matters. It can be very lonely not being able to relate to people because they have only book knowledge of religion or philosophy or no interest at all, and it was apparent to me that very few apply what spiritual knowledge they profess to believe. There are some people who are not prepared, or perhaps are afraid, to open their minds to anything new. I felt the emotional freedom to keep on with my investigations.

I went to a 'Spiritual Day', which was a gathering held in a huge hall at Turangawaewae, the name of the official residence and grounds of the then Maori queen, located in Ngaruawahia, a country town near Hamilton.

I sat down on the steps just inside the entrance door of a huge hall to observe the different activities that were going on. About 30 people were sitting in chairs facing to the right towards three women standing on a stage. One of the women stepped forward and began speaking into a microphone.

'That man down there.' She pointed in my direction. 'Yes, you, sir; may I come to you? You are going to go to India, and you will meet Sai Baba. Don't worry, the money to go is coming.' The woman had spoken with such conviction that I was stunned. There must be some mistake.

The small gathering broke up soon afterwards and so I stood up to walk away. The woman who had given me the message approached me: 'I knew as soon as I saw you that you were going to go to India,' she said. I was surprised that she had heard of Sai Baba. She seemed happy for me, but how could I afford the fare to get to India? Currently, I was unwaged. However, I felt emotionally uplifted but bewildered.

A few months afterwards, my stepfather George died and he left me the legacy first predicted 35 years ago. When I next visited Marie, I asked her opinion: 'If Sai Baba has a presence everywhere because he is not limited by the physical world, and he is aware of everything — is it really necessary to travel to India to see him in the flesh?'

'I can see him nodding his head,' said Marie unceremoniously. 'Yes, go.' Later, Nancy and Peter also told me that Sai Baba was encouraging me to go.

A healers' meeting

I arranged for several people to meet at Rebecca's home, including Marie and a Maori traditional healer. There were nine people present. Joy had once again given vague reasons for not wanting to attend. The Maori healer talked extensively about his experiences healing and the treatments that he used, including using native plants. He took control of the meeting from the beginning and performed several traditional prayers and blessings in Maori. I had arranged for us to meet so that everyone could share their healing knowledge and personal experiences, and so I became unsettled because the other people present were not being invited to exchange experiences — the Maori healer was treating this gathering as if it were a lecture and a demonstration of Maori culture.

I glanced at Marie. She appeared to be very calm and serene, and often said: 'Isn't that marvellous!' as she listened to the healer's presentation. She had no ego. I had explained to her when I invited her that it could be a great day of swapping knowledge and learning from each other. When I had first met Marie, she had stressed that I should not be reluctant to discuss my thoughts with her because we could all learn from each other. The Maori healer did not ask anyone else for their input. I tried hard to be calm, but I had been looking forward to all of us sharing our knowledge and had especially wanted to hear about Marie's experiences. I was sitting beside her when we took a break for refreshments. She seemed content to sit quietly, but I was still struggling to relax. We did not speak at first, but then unexpectedly Marie spoke without looking at me.

'Yes. You were my son. I have almost finished handing you over to Sai Baba.' I realised that it appeared to be White Eagle speaking. Marie then continued to sit quietly making no further comment, as if nothing unusual had happened because she paid me no attention. I had never mentioned anything to Marie suggesting that I had ever been White Eagle's son. If there was to be any 'handover' from White Eagle to Sai Baba, I had previously supposed that Sai Baba would override White Eagle when necessary, but there may have been unseen spiritual adjustments to be made, or spiritual advancement required of me, and that apparently had taken about two years since I had decided on Sai Baba as my spiritual master. I had been told that Marie did not always remember the content of White Eagle's messages; the information was meant for the listener and may not be remembered by the human 'instrument' that delivered the message. Francie Williams had said that she did not remember much about the personal readings that she did.

One week earlier I had been at Marie's house. She had asked me if I would please give her healing because of a terrible pain in her eye. Today the Maori healer heard her tell me that a small amount of pain had returned. He offered to help her, and applied healing in a similar way to how I had been taught.

I received an appreciative typed letter in the mail from Marie two days later. She thanked me for the healing that I had given her because the pain in her eye had initially gone after I gave her healing. A little pain returned later, she said, but after the Maori healer applied healing, the remaining pain had gone. I think that Marie may have been remembering how Joy had been upset by what she probably felt was a reprimand by White Eagle. Marie may have wanted to make sure that I was not feeling that I had been put in the shade by the Maori healer.

Tickets to India

I decided that I *would* travel to India, so in early March 2001 I started to prepare. I did feel a little ridiculous that I was going to follow through on the suggestions to travel that I had been given — that Sai Baba was expecting me. Some Indian friends told me that there was information on the internet about Sai Baba's travel movements. The site advised that visitors should be at the ashram before the end of March because Sai Baba leaves the ashram to go to a cooler area during the summer months. However, my passport had expired, and it could not be renewed in time for me to leave before the end of March. I would have to be patient and go to India towards the end of the year; I was certain that I would get there when it was spiritually appropriate. I was bubbling with anticipation.

In September I went to a travel agent who was familiar with arranging for travellers to go to Sai Baba's ashram. He was booking me on a flight to Bangalore airport in South India when the phone rang; people from a privately-run spiritual class had previously asked the travel agent to organise all transport and accommodation necessary for them from Auckland to Sai Baba's ashram in a desert village, stopping overnight in Bangalore. Sai Baba's ashram was 150 kilometres further north, a two-and-a-half-hour drive by car. I could join their party so that we would all save money on expenses. By this stage I was certain that I was receiving spiritual assistance!

My Indian friends told me that I would be able to be accommodated at Sai Baba's ashram beside the small village where he was born. I would have to be up early and out the door at 4 am to go and queue up to wait for Sai Baba, who would arrive for darshan three hours later. 'Darshan' means having a blessed sight of a holy person or holy image; devotees could personally *see* Sai Baba.

I had messages from mediums and clairvoyants prior to leaving for India. I was told that Mum and Dad supported my trip, and I began to regularly receive other encouraging messages. They both had died 15 years earlier. A clairvoyant woman that headed a meditation group told me that my trip to India would be trouble-free because she had been shown eagle wings. She also said that White Eagle presented me with a bearskin cloak 'to keep me warm'. On a different day, another clairvoyant woman repeated the bearskin message. Did the cloak symbolise a Native American Indian tradition? The messages seemed to mean that I would be spiritually protected.

As I was preparing to leave for India, I was looking at the most recently taken aura photograph of myself. I decided to hold the photograph directly in front of me in the bright sunlight; would the result be the same as my earlier experiments looking in the mirror? I focused on the photograph while keeping my mind still, and then closed my eyes. I expected to see the shape of my head and shoulders in colour. I waited for about 20 seconds until I clearly saw a blue sky with layers of puffy white clouds moving from right to left very quickly, then thinning out until there was only a wisp of cloud remaining high in 'the sky'. I had learned from various clairvoyants that as far as images in people's auras go, the right side shows what influences are coming up over the next few weeks or months. Are my positive experiences going to increase? Am I going to have greater awareness? One week earlier I had spoken to a woman who operated an aura camera. She had explained how she used her psychic capability professionally; she would close her eyes and see her client either relaxing or performing some activity on a beach. She would then have to interpret that information to advise the client. Maybe I could develop a similar system.

A similar type of meditation gradually became normal for me over the coming years — perhaps it could be called an in-body meditation. Peter had told me that was the method that Sai Baba 'encourages'. Because I had trained myself to temporarily free my mind from thinking when necessary, I had probably become more receptive to connecting to akashic influences. Over the following years I often had an almost immediate result — without warning I can receive information without having asked any question.

Chapter 13
At Sai Baba's ashram, October 2001

Settling in

TWELVE MONTHS AFTER RECEIVING THE MESSAGE that I would meet Sai Baba, I arrived at Bangalore with my travelling companions. It was night-time. At the airport exit I had to cling to my bags as men insisted that they were the ones sent to collect us, but our group leader located the pre-arranged driver, and soon we were weaving through the bustling traffic to a small hotel where we spent the night. The next morning, we departed for the ashram after a satisfying buffet breakfast, driven by the same driver from the day before accompanied by his assistant. Seven of us scrambled into the Jeep-type small vehicle; the driver's assistant sat on top of the luggage. We squeezed our way through the bustling continuously tooting traffic that must have been keeping to their own flexible lanes with imaginary gaps in the traffic that the driver could take advantage of. When we commenced our journey there appeared to be three lanes in the city, but five rows of traffic.

We arrived at the village of Puttaparthi after a two-and-a-half-hour trip along good roads. This was where Sai Baba had been born. In the days when he was a youth but already famous, this trip had been quite an ordeal because the roads were atrocious; a river had to be crossed if it was the wet season but determined people had still been willing to travel long distances to see Sai Baba. It was obvious that since then the small remote village had undergone a lot of development. The book written by Howard Murphet had instigated a worldwide interest in Sai Baba. Blocks of new apartments had been built and some were for sale. There were crowds of visitors and dozens of three-wheeled taxis on the streets. The ashram was surrounded by high walls, but the entrance was open. I was told that the gates were closed after the evening meal.

A street scene beside Sai Baba's Ashram entrance

There were many buildings inside the ashram; in old photographs that I had seen, there was only a mandir — the temple — and a large old house nearby. The devotees had to sit and sometimes sleep overnight on the ground. Howard and Iris had stayed in the house as Sai Baba's guests. Because the number of visitors to the ashram had grown over the years, it had been necessary to provide more amenities.

At the reception area inside the ashram, our group reported to some old dignified-looking men lounging at a long table. They gave the impression that they were very tired or uninterested in welcoming new arrivals. They were, however, not unpleasant. Maybe this duty was their retirement service, or maybe they were exhausted from talking to the endless stream of new arrivals. We paid about 10 dollars each to stay for 10 days. I needed to stay for 14 days with my tour group. I renewed my application when it expired.

I was directed to a pathway that led to a large hall at the end of a row of halls at the far end of the ashram — the halls were called sheds by the organisers. A creature like a gecko raced ahead of me, wobbling from side to side like a pacing horse. Small pieces of marble were scattered on top of the paths that were not paved. I saw buses with palm branches tied to them drive along the larger pathways to deposit their passengers — some devotees had travelled from Bihar state, 2100 kilometres to the north and 40 hours' driving.

I was to be sharing the accommodation shed with Western males only — that meant any men from outside India, including those of Indian heritage. Families from within India could stay together in the other sheds but there was a separate shed for Western women. There were no cooking facilities in the men's shed, and toilets and showers were passably clean. Our toilets were a big improvement over the public toilets, which often had a putrefying stench wafting around them, but I was to see them being cleaned on a regular basis. Two grey-haired, sad-looking stray dogs slept on the entrance porch to our shed and several pigeons fluttered around. A few large monkeys and their offspring seemed unafraid of people and nibbled on something as they congregated nearby.

I returned to the village outside the ashram, hired a mattress and bought a fold-up stretcher to avoid sleeping on the wooden floor. I was 61 years old and not supple. I initially shared the shed with four men: from Russia, Japan, Croatia, and Sri Lanka, but as the days passed, more men kept arriving to join us. Sai Baba's birthday was coming up on the 23rd of November, and I was told there would be a huge number of devotees arriving daily as that day got closer, and there would be devotees crowding together shoulder to shoulder at darshan. It was now the 28th of October 2001.

The electricity officially ceased at 9 pm every night. Power for the village outside and for the ashram was supplied by generators. We were made aware that soap was to be avoided to keep the underground water table as pure as possible; I saw a car getting washed without using soap. Immaculately groomed cars occasionally parked outside an official-looking building and appeared to be from some government agencies; they were usually Hindustan Imperials that looked like the 1953 Austin A70 that my father had once owned in 1956, but there were several late-model Japanese cars as well.

Spiritual Tasering

I already knew a few basic facts about Sai Baba. By the end of the twentieth century Sai Baba was 74 years old; the ashram where he was based had been constructed many years before on land provided by the government. There is an original tiny mandir — a temple — which was still standing in the small village outside the ashram, but it had quickly proved to be too small to house all the devotees of the then 22-year-old Sathya Sai Baba. The new ashram grew so large over the following years that it could house hundreds of visitors who needed accommodation, and there was room inside the walls to allow thousands of devotees to congregate. Sai Baba travelled around the villages in the region regularly, but usually returned in the afternoon to walk around his devotees gathered at the ashram. Previous famous avatars in Indian history were Rama and Krishna. Jesus, the Buddha, and Shirdi Sai Baba are also regarded as avatars by many Indians.

I had not been able to sleep until after 10 pm, but I awoke the first morning at 3 am — I heard water splashing because someone was taking a shower. I soon did the same because the urge not to delay was strong; I was surprised to feel a thrill of anticipation in my heart. I dressed in the thin white cotton clothing that I had bought in a charity shop because I had seen photographs of all the devotees wearing white. It was probably about 15° Celsius when I finished dressing, but I was certain that it was going to be hot soon. I left the shed just after half-past three to go to queue up outside the mandir, where I had been told Sai Baba would be arriving later for darshan.

As I left the Western men's shed and walked along the dirt pathway there were several Indian men standing silently with shawls draped over their shoulders and with woollen beanies on their heads. I could see candles flickering through the open doors of the sheds and rows of people lay on the floors. About a dozen people, including several Westerners, were heading in the direction of the mandir — a 10-minute walk away. A crow was intermittently squawking and flapping about in one of the palm trees beside the pathway. I found myself automatically hurrying along with a sense of purpose, but I felt relaxed and looking forward to an interesting day. Why should I expect to have a personal spiritual experience? I would soon be but one person among the thousands that will be congregating.

I walked along the footpaths that ran between the sheds, and eventually arrived at a wider concreted alleyway. As I passed a windowless building, I could hear people working inside, probably preparing breakfast, which was going to be about 9 am. There was now a sprinkling of people all heading towards the mandir, which was now about 200 metres ahead.

Suddenly, a fierce vibration about the size of a football in and around the centre of my chest overwhelmed me. I gasped and sobbed involuntarily as I was compelled to bend over. Tears poured down my cheeks and I could not breathe because I felt paralysed. The vibrating force seemed to extend out in front of me. I felt certain that this must be a psychic/spiritual force, although I did not understand at the time what the reason for it was. The shaking eased off after about 10 seconds and the force gradually subsided; I could breathe comfortably. I immediately took my pulse because I wanted to keep recording evidence; it was 64 beats per minute — within my usual heart-rate range. I was confident that my heart was not going to explode. I was amazed but not worried. I remembered that the past few years had been a period of investigation and recording of spiritual experiences, like a science project. Now I had it. Immediately I had a feeling of satisfaction and relief that my journey to India was already proving worthwhile in a way that I would never have imagined. My body may perhaps have been triggered to release tensions and stresses, but I was not to consider that possibility until later. My mind had become overwhelmed because of the implausibility of what had happened; it was numb.

I did not forget, even for a minute, my determination to try to prove that there is a spiritual ladder. One of my motives for writing this book is to inform readers about methods that worked for me and may help others.

Obviously, it is your genuine intention combined with willpower and persistence that will register in an appropriate dimension. Finally, I had evidence that what I had heard from other people about being moved physically by an unseen force was true. Even Joy had told me that she had been physically steered into a shop on one occasion; she then spotted an artist's impression of Jesus, which she bought. There was no need to worry that this experience was caused by anything negative because as Joy and Peter had informed me, why should it be anything but positive for me if I pray to be protected and I am a good person? Also, was it true that Sai Baba had encouraged me to come?

A minute later I had recovered my composure and hobbled onwards slowly — I did not want to draw attention to myself; if I had, an observer might reasonably think that I had had a heart attack. It would be many years before I was to consider that my kundalini must have been activated by an electro-spiritual force. For the student of occultism, the kundalini has been called the 'World Mother' — the Buddhi considered as an active instead of a passive principle.

I joined about a dozen men in a queue sitting quietly on some steps that led up a hill away from the mandir. Many more men began to arrive and join the queue. 'Where are you from?' whispered the curious young Indian man sitting in front of me.

Soon we were shepherded by volunteers into about 12 parallel rows, with about 15 people in each row. It appeared that we had to wait for permission to enter the enclosed area that was in front of the mandir, which was surrounded by a low wall but was open-sided and covered by a high ceiling.

The Mandir at Puttiparti

The entrance gates were opened at 4 am and dozens of men and women hurried inside from the village. When I met some of those people later, they told me that they preferred to rent temporary accommodation in the village instead of staying in the ashram. It was more convenient for them to buy food whenever they liked and cook for themselves if they wanted to. For some visitors, the vegetarian meals available in the ashram restaurants may not have been to their liking.

Later, I was informed that 13,000 people could fit into the enclosed area where everyone would sit waiting for darshan. The floor had large black marble tiles laid in a concave shape, very gently sloping towards the mandir at the front. This enabled everyone to have a clear view of the proceedings that took place. There was almost total silence.

I ended up sitting cross-legged about four rows from the front of an aisle. Tears started to roll down my cheeks; why, I do not know. Now it seemed as if the impossible was soon going to happen. What I had hoped for, that I would fortify my understanding that Sai Baba was really a genuine guru, a spiritual master, seemed to be coming true, and I was obviously completely emotionally overcome. My mind still seemed to be numb — I did not seem to be thinking.

As more people kept entering and sitting behind us, youthful volunteers in the aisles assisted with the crowd control, quietly using hand signals to indicate that we should move closer together by inching forward. We were packed in like sardines in a tin, 'as only the Indians can', Howard Murphet had said in his book. I had to keep moving the position of my legs every few minutes because I had deteriorating hip joints and lower-back problems. I was in constant pain during the next four hours. To complicate matters, I got cramp in my legs every few minutes.

A delegation of European men from Ireland, all wearing green scarves, were sitting next to me. The closest of them briefly put his arm around my shoulders to comfort me when I explained that I was unable to stop crying. 'Don't worry; we understand,' he said sympathetically. I could now relate to people who had been in similar situations and had experiences that proved the existence of spiritual or psychic forces and were overwhelmed. My lifelong hope that there were genuine spiritual masters alive in the modern era was becoming a reality. What came to mind was an incident in the Christian Bible when a man called Saul heard a voice but saw no one, and he was blinded for three days by a light from above and did not eat or drink for those three days. I could not verify whether that story was true, but what had just happened to me on the way here definitely was. My tears stopped after about half an hour.

Sai Baba had a routine that I was to find he followed every day. He always entered at an entrance opposite to the men where all the women had filed through from their own entrance and were seated together. He then moved very slowly through the aisles and passed by the men, finishing up climbing a few steps onto the veranda that ran along the front of the mandir. About 20 men were already sitting there cross-legged. They always arrived later than most of the devotees; they entered through a small side entrance. I presumed that some of them needed more time sleeping because of their responsibilities: teachers, doctors from the two hospitals, lecturers from the various educational schools, and visiting dignitaries. Much later, several dozen school children filed in through the same small side entrance and sat directly in front of the veranda. All the men and the children present wore all-white clothing, and everyone entering any building on the ashram left their sandals outside.

Except for occasional whispering, all was quiet until 5 am when instructions were given by an elderly man who moved systematically along the aisles, briefly explaining what the procedure was and a few rules we were expected to follow. He spoke in Telugu at first, the language of this state, Andhra Pradesh, and a major language of southern India spoken by 75 million people. He repeated the address in English. He said that when Sai Baba comes, we should stay seated. Ten minutes later various activities commenced. A group of about 20 men arrived and chanted together for about 10 minutes in front of a structure that I could not see properly; this must have been a traditional ceremony. About 20 women passed by outside at 6 am singing boisterously, and five minutes later, on the opposite end of the mandir, a group of men walked slowly past, singing enthusiastically. Above our heads a few pigeons wriggled and fluttered as they jumped around the masses of exposed electrical wiring that crisscrossed the ceiling. Dawn was now breaking.

When Sai Baba appeared at 7 am everyone was immediately fully alert, and a buzz of excitement rippled through the waiting crowd. Pleasant recorded instrumental Indian music was relayed over speakers as Sai Baba strolled very slowly around the women's aisles, sometimes pausing briefly to say a few words. As he passed along the aisles, he encountered a few devotees' outstretched hands waving letters in front of him, most of which he accepted and gathered into his spare hand. Over the next few days, I had decided on an appropriate question that I would like an answer to, so I scribbled it on a piece of paper that I had ripped off a full sheet. I had meant to rewrite it tidily but had been so relaxed between darshans after being 'zapped' that I had little interest in doing so. Sometimes people would stand up after he had spoken to them and they would then walk towards the veranda. These were people that he must have invited to go and wait for him until he had completed his darshan because they had been granted an interview with him. Other people would often stand up and join the chosen person, apparently because they were all part of the same family or group.

Sai Baba did not look my way at all as I waited for nine morning darshans and for several afternoon darshans. Every day I was in almost constant agony as I sat attempting to sit cross-legged; the pain had to be endured. I was in such an unusual mental state that I was not concerned about anything from the past or what may happen in the future; I was focused on *now*. I did not allow the persistent pain and discomfort to deter me from my mission to meet Sai Baba. When I first noticed my mental attitude, I thought that it was very curious — there was a strange feeling of anticipation and excitement in my heart area constantly, but my mind was at peace. I had not even considered that I should stop attending darshan because of my physical pains.

Every day there was a similar routine after Sai Baba had completed his darshan at 8 am. More than half of the crowd dispersed; the rest stayed seated. A small very professional-sounding orchestra accompanied the devotees who stayed to sing bhajans. It became obvious that almost everyone was familiar with the bhajans, but I did not recognise most of them.

I was told that most of Sai Baba's public discourses were given in Telugu. Sai Baba spoke very quickly without pauses on the DVDs of his discourses that I had viewed. His words were immediately interpreted into English, and he abruptly corrected any rare inaccurate interpretation.

The author with several volunteers, 2001

I started a daily routine, staying on for a while after darshan. Being part of such a large group singing in unison was enthralling. Many of those present had come from other Indian states, and some were from other countries. There were several Buddhist monks from Nepal and Sri Lanka, and a few Muslims. Some Sikhs were among the volunteers. There were a few European Africans and a sprinkling of devotees from Japan and Taiwan. Breakfast was available in a nearby building if I did not delay too long after darshan, and lunch and an evening meal were also available each day.

Puja (worship); another zapping

It was common to see a small group of perhaps 10 people arrive at the ashram and gather around portable food containers, then sit on the bare ground to eat. Travelling by train is cheap in India, so the poor could afford to travel occasionally. The meals at the ashram restaurants cost about 50 to 80 rupees, or two or three New Zealand dollars, but the poorest Indian devotees could collect food coupons from a coupon office.

The third day, after darshan, a queue of men had formed in front of the mandir. 'Excuse me. Do you know what the queue is for?' I asked a young man. I was lucky; he spoke English.

'Puja for Westerners,' he told me.

Puja? I had read the word in Howard Murphet's book. I could not remember what it meant but I wanted to see inside the mandir. Every morning the group of men arriving for darshan after 6 am entered through the side door, then went into the mandir building. Very faint muffled singing or chanting could be heard for half an hour. When the men came out, they sat cross-legged on the veranda in front of the mandir and waited there for darshan.

I decided to go into the mandir. As the men at the front of the queue went through a plastic curtain screen at the entrance, other men were continually brushing past them coming out. As I got to the door I was suddenly gasping for breath because my chest was vigorously shaking and vibrating again! I hesitated momentarily because it was difficult to move my legs. The shaking was severe and I struggled to breathe, but after pausing, I continued to go inside. Some tears flowed briefly. The men in front of me were prostrating in front of a life-sized picture of Sathya Sai Baba alongside a similar-sized picture of Shirdi Sai Baba, an Indian saint who had died 80 years previously. Sathya Sai Baba was reported to have refused to attend school when he was 13 years old. He insisted that he was Shirdi Sai Baba reborn, and he had to attend to his devotees. Sathya Sai Baba had gradually become much revered by millions of people.

I was so awed at my condition that I had no hesitation in humbly prostrating myself, because I had been subjected to an overwhelming force once again. I left the mandir immediately afterwards, following the men that had preceded me. Any pride that I may have had was overcome by the after-effects of the powerful force that had engulfed me. Observing the interior of the mandir had become irrelevant because everything had become a blur to me. There had been no thought involved in my actions inside the mandir.

Thai massage

There was a two-storeyed building that housed one of the ashram restaurants on the ground floor. At 11 am daily there were 'Talks for Westerners' in a large hall on the first floor. The first time I attended, an Indian pundit speedily reeled off a comprehensive talk about an ancient scripture without referring to any notes. I found the extent of his knowledge incredible.

Men continued to arrive to stay at the Westerners' shed as the days went by until it was becoming crowded. Sai Baba's birthday was only about two weeks away. I was told that there would be a continual increase in the number of devotees arriving — the ashram would be packed shoulder to shoulder by the day of Baba's birthday.

'The Sheds', inside Sai Baba's ashram, 2001

There were three restaurants in the ashram: one with North Indian food, one with South Indian food, and the so-called 'Westerners'' restaurant that nevertheless had Indian flavours. All meals were vegetarian. I found that I was not hungry most days because of my unusual state of mind — I did not want any conversation or entertainment and had little appetite, but I tried to eat something to keep my strength up.

My legs, hips and back became so stiff that after a few days I had trouble walking. Sitting for four hours or more daily on the floor squirming around in pain at darshan was crippling me. Fortunately for me, by chance I sat next to an American masseur at breakfast one morning. He said that he had tried all the massage parlours in the village and the dearest or cleanest were not the best. He suggested that I go to an Indian masseur who had rooms nearby in the village; he used a Thai massage method and was the best local masseur, but his premises were unattractive.

I did as the American suggested, and immediately hobbled along to the recommended masseur. His small premises did appear drab, and he and his female assistant appeared to be unsophisticated. The masseur covered my body in oil, including my head, and his technique was very forceful and energetic, but he was trying to look congenial as he worked because his knowledge of English was poor. He squeezed my hands and toes so hard and rubbed my head and body so vigorously that I was worried he would split my skin.

I could hardly believe it when my hips and back felt pain-free and flexible again by the next morning.

A third zapping

On the tenth day after morning darshan was over, there was a queue outside the mandir again. 'What's the queue for today?' I asked a man nearby.

'Meditation for Westerners,' he replied. That could be interesting, and so I joined the queue. Since I had received the first 'zapping' I felt so calm and stress-free that I had not left the ashram at all. I had read that Sai Baba said we should remember why we were here; were we here to tour around and buy cheap trinkets from the tourist shops out in the village, or were we here for spiritual gold? However, the warm feeling around my heart had diminished and I had started to feel restless, as if my presence at the ashram was no longer spiritually necessary. My previously wandering mind had been so overcome by amazement that it had stopped thinking of anything but what I had been experiencing the last 10 days.

I had no reason to expect that I would be zapped again, so I was astonished when it did happen again as I went through the mandir doorway. This time the vibration was much less than the previous times, but it was again like an electric shock in my heart and chest muscles. I concentrated on breathing and recovered quickly; there were no tears.

The meditation session in the mandir lasted half an hour. I had been so surprised at my latest zapping that my mind was buzzing. I being singled out again — why?

Was the prophecy correct?

When I arrived at darshan the next morning, I was disappointed to see that dozens of devotees had arrived before me although it was well before 4 am. I was certain that I could not be included in the first group that would go into darshan. There were already about a dozen rows lined up, so I was astounded when one extra row was added, and I was immediately directed into it. Before I could get over thinking how incredible that was, my line of devotees was on the move and the row that I was in was going into the mandir enclosure first! I was dumbfounded. The prophecy must be coming true. I started to feel very apprehensive because I *knew* now that this was certainly the day that I would meet Sai Baba; I had no doubts. I had an excited feeling in my heart. No — it was more like being afraid, very afraid.

I decided not to think about where to sit. I used my intuition and sat down near to where I had entered, because there was a continuous flow of people behind me. I was positioned beside an aisle in the front row. Immediately I was in continual pain again. I had already endured more than 36 hours of pain sitting and waiting to meet Sai Baba as prophesied.

As usual, I had a pen and a small pocket diary with me. Most days I had not felt like writing anything while I waited because it seemed irrelevant and a distraction. I became aware that now, for some inexplicable reason, I had become very calm. Was this the calm before the storm? As I waited, I discreetly made brief notes in my diary about the atmosphere and what I was witnessing.

The recorded Indian music announcing Sai Baba's approach started playing at the usual time. He entered the building followed by two youths crouching low on their haunches. As usual, there was a buzz of excitement from the devotees.

Suddenly, my facial muscles and my cheeks were shaking up and down and my chest muscles had begun to jump violently. This reaction was unexpected and alarming! There was a feeling like terror in my chest, and tears suddenly started to stream down my face. My cheeks, heart, and chest muscles continued to vibrate uncontrollably; I felt as if I were receiving a continuous electric current. At last, I was about to have what must be the most important meeting of my life and Sai Baba would see right through me! He would probably know all my frailties; there would be nowhere to hide. I was concerned that I must look an emotional mess.

Sai Baba took the usual route through the excited throng, stopping to take some letters as usual. The devotees sat bolt upright on their haunches at Sai Baba's approach. Some in the front row were on their knees as he approached to speak to them. He chatted here and there, and I saw him trickle vibhuti from his fingers across several outstretched hands. Forty-five minutes later he had arrived within 15 metres from where I waited.

Two old Englishmen positioned next to me had been excitedly whispering for over four hours but had not acknowledged me in any way. Sai Baba had his back to me and was declining to accept a proffered offering. The devotee moved back to the third row, looking very dejected. Sai Baba half turned as if casually glancing around, and then his gaze appeared to be riveted on me. I was stunned to see him ignore the many people near him and break out into an enormous smile and hurry in my direction. I knew that he was heading towards me. I felt terrified but relieved and grateful. I made a tremendous effort to control my tears and tried to brush them away with a quick swipe of my right hand; the thousands of devotees would all have their eyes on me in a few seconds and I was still continuously receiving small shocks to my face and chest and all the muscles were vibrating crazily.

Suddenly, inexplicably, the vibrations stopped.

'Where are you from?' Sai Baba asked immediately, as he arrived in front of me. He leaned over as he spoke, and casually took the note that I held out for him and added it to the other letters that he held in his other hand. I was surprised and briefly unsettled, because I had not expected him to stop after taking the note. Sai Baba was now holding my tatty scrap of paper and I felt ashamed, but he had not immediately moved on. He had stopped to speak to me and so I had to answer him.

'New Zealand,' I said.

'I beg your pardon?' said Sai Baba.

'New Zealand!' I said a little louder.

'Oh, New Zealand!' Then Sai Baba paused. 'How many?'

I guessed that this must mean how many people were accompanying me today.

'Just me,' I responded, wondering if that signified that I was a loner. Sai Baba wore a glorious smile and his eyes were gleaming as if he was extremely pleased to meet me. Then he said, as he waved his hand, 'Go!' and turned away to continue with his darshan.

I sat there, feeling confused. What did that mean? In the book that Marie had given me, Sai Baba had said 'Go!' when he was inviting a devotee for an interview. But he had already 'met' me, as had been predicted in New Zealand. Was I being invited for an interview? What should I do now? After a brief hesitation, I made some small movements so that I would appear to be getting ready to move, but I did not know where to move to.

'Stay there!' This whispered order came from the crouching youth following immediately behind Sai Baba. As Sai Baba moved further away, the youth said urgently, 'Go now!' He gestured in the direction of the veranda steps nearby.

Feeling relieved, I stood up and walked off in the opposite direction to Sai Baba. My face had started shaking uncontrollably again. I had to pass between the thousands of devotees surrounding the aisles. Somehow, I was guided on to the veranda, where an elderly man patted the floor next to him: 'Sit here,' he said.

The interview

About 15 minutes later, the people who had been granted an interview were gathered in a large room that led off the veranda. The room had no furniture except one armchair. Women sat on the polished wooden floor on one side and men sat opposite. I counted 15 people in all; I wanted to remember all the details. Sai Baba entered the room about 10 minutes later carrying the letters, which he placed in a wire basket.

'How are you?' he asked loudly. He looked relaxed as he moved between the two groups of people.

'Happy! Happy!' said a few people in unison.

'How are you?' Sai Baba asked again, but more querulously.

'Happy! Happy!' a few extra people answered this time.

'No, sir. Your wife is not happy,' said Sai Baba, addressing an elderly man.

One of the women started sobbing. 'You are worried about your son,' said Sai Baba matter-of-factly. He then asked some of the people where they were from. The man next to me said that he was from Atlanta. I was sitting in a corner, silently crying tears of relief. My muscles had stopped vibrating while I was sitting on the veranda.

I had always had an unquenchable yearning that there should be someone that could speak genuine spiritual truth to people. It was now apparent that Sai Baba was such a person. I already had a wonderful circle of friends in New Zealand that I thought were humble and special, but Sai Baba was extraordinary. It was now obvious to me that sometimes there are spiritual masters on earth; people who are in harmony with the knowledge of the akasha and even greater knowledge that was usually beyond the senses. I was relieved that I had found this was true, after my whole life wanting to have it confirmed. Yes, there *was* the 'divine' knowledge available that I had always believed in.

A distinguished-looking old Indian man, who was probably in his late eighties or even perhaps in his nineties, entered the room. Sai Baba tried to prevent the man from humbly kneeling to touch his feet, but without success. The old man carried a stethoscope, and after standing up, he used it to quickly examine Sai Baba, who cheerfully acquiesced to the insistent probing. 'He is a very great man,' said Sai Baba reverently after the old man had hurried away.

Sai Baba chatted to various individuals in the room, and from time to time he escorted people to another room, returning with them after a few minutes. I was emotionally drained; tears had restarted and were flowing down my cheeks. At first, I was not focusing on the various conversations, but I eventually rallied my thoughts: I should start to take more notice of what was happening. The tears stopped. Sai Baba spoke to a young Indian woman from England who was sitting at the front of the women's group. I heard the woman say 'Shiva Shakti' and suddenly Sai Baba had a large gold-coloured medallion swinging from his hand by a chain that was a similar colour. There were surprised exclamations from the people watching. Two figures were embossed on the medallion, a male and a female. 'What do they mean to you?' Sai Baba asked, as he placed it around the woman's neck.

'Positive and negative,' was the reply.

Sai Baba gave a small nod. I could hardly believe what had happened.

Sai Baba then said a few words to another woman. I missed hearing what was said because I was still recovering my wits, but then I was startled to see that there was another gold-coloured chain dangling from Sai Baba's outstretched hand. It was slimmer, more delicate than the first chain, and the attached medallion was smaller. It stopped swinging and Sai Baba lowered the chain over the woman's head. She adjusted it so that it fitted comfortably around her neck.

'You have trouble with your ring, sir?' Sai Baba had moved to stand in front of the man from Atlanta. I did not hear an answer. Sai Baba moved on and spoke to the woman who had been sobbing earlier. 'Don't worry about your son: mental trouble. I will look after him.'

What I saw next was almost unbelievable. There was a silvery decorated vessel, the size and shape of a half-litre jug, sitting on

Sai Baba's outstretched palm. Several people gasped: it had appeared out of nowhere. Sai Baba lifted its lid. I heard him say, 'Three times a day,' as he passed the vessel to the woman. Later I wondered if it had contained vibhuti.

There had been a buzz of astonishment from the small crowd, but Sai Baba showed no pride of accomplishment. He brushed off praise as if what he did was of no consequence. The book about him that I had read said he told people that the gifts that 'materialise' are demonstrating God's love. 'The gifts help to build faith. They are not 'miracles', he said.

A woman spoke to Sai Baba after he sat down briefly on the chair. He then reached for the basket holding the letters that he had been handed during darshan and dipped his hand in without looking at what he was grasping. He examined the unopened envelope that he had lifted out. He seemed to know that it was from the woman. He had a brief chat with her, then escorted her to the other room.

Sai Baba soon returned, and he stood near me facing the man from Atlanta.

'Give me your ring, sir,' he said calmly, as he held out his hand.

The man from Atlanta removed his ring and passed it over. Sai Baba took it in both hands and cupped them together around the ring. He looked lovingly between his palms while he blew gently three times on the ring, then passed it back to the man. I could see a large blue stone mounted on it. 'Blue for peace,' said Sai Baba.

When he had moved on and chosen a group of people to take for a private interview, I questioned the man with the ring.

'Why did he do that?' I was now feeling very peaceful and relaxed. For some reason, my tears had stopped.

'Sai Baba materialised that ring for me three years ago. It developed a large crack.' He showed me where he had put sticking plaster on his finger to protect it from being chafed. 'Now there is no crack, and there's a blue stone on top that wasn't there before!'

When Sai Baba returned to the room, he looked in my direction and gestured towards our corner group.

'Come, sir.' Sai Baba must be looking at the man on my left. I glanced left. Sai Baba saw that I could not believe that he had indicated me.

'No, you, sir!' He *was* pointing at me.

Unprepared, I staggered to my feet, and Sai Baba ushered me past a curtain into the other room. What should I do now? For some reason I had not been expecting to be invited for a private interview. There was a couch on the far side, and an armchair and a desk to the left. I took a few steps forward, but I was not going to sit down and leave Sai Baba standing. My mind felt blank — perhaps it was numb. I had been caught completely by surprise. Here was the chance of a lifetime and no questions came to mind.

'Bhakta, you worry too much,' said Sai Baba. As I turned around to face him, he slowly walked past me and crossed the room, looking thoughtful. He seemed in no hurry.

'Sometimes depression. Be happy!' He said this in a relaxed, conversational way.

Sai Baba then said, 'Sometimes you think that you should get married, and sometimes you think that you shouldn't. Don't get married — wife trouble!' I had not asked or answered any question. Sai Baba looked calm and untroubled. 'Don't worry about other people. Other people — jealous,' he said thoughtfully. Then he said, 'Got a pen?'

I was surprised by the question. 'Yes,' I replied. I took the pen from my pocket. At last, I had spoken!

Sai Baba moved to the desk and picked up a clipboard, glanced at it, and then passed it to me. He pointed to the bottom of the business letter that was clamped onto it. 'Put address.'

I now felt very calm. With a steady hand I had no trouble to neatly print my home address. Sai Baba took the clipboard and examined what I had printed. He nodded, and then returned the clipboard to the desk.

'And you are by yourself?'

I assured him that I was.

'What! No gang?' he remarked with a wry smile.

'Just me,' I said.

'Time,' said Sai Baba, after a short pause. 'We will talk again.'

He walked around to the front of the desk and moved away just as I moved forward. He stopped suddenly and swung around, causing one of his fingers to brush one of mine. He then slowly escorted me towards the door.

'Time. We will talk again,' he repeated.

I was the last person to be invited for a meeting, or 'interview'. I had never expected anything more than to 'meet' Sai Baba. Sai Baba handed out small plastic packets of vibhuti to everyone before they left. As he was passing me a handful — later I counted nine packets — I mustered up the courage to ask him a question, because now I felt very anxious. I did not want to be disrespectful, but I felt that I had to interrupt Baba; my heart was in my mouth.

'Baba, I didn't write my name!' Was I demonstrating a lack of confidence in Sai Baba's ability to be aware of that? Did he need to know my name? Had he even needed my letter?

'I know,' he responded immediately without looking at me, as he continued passing out the packets of vibhuti.

After I left the mandir, I kept to myself for an hour or so. That was Sai Baba's recommendation — according to information in a book about him — so that the full importance of our meeting was not lost. Positive energy was dissipated by unnecessary talking, he has said in the past.

What had I written in my letter? What had been my final decision about what was the important question that I wanted to ask Sai Baba's help with? It was this: 'How can I love people more?' That was the most important question that I could think of. I never wanted to have any feelings of anger, envy, jealousy, regret, or guilt; there was no option — if I wanted to be genuinely peaceful — but to forgive other people's faults and my own. Alternate questions could have been about attempting to solve fleeting problems that were not going to have a long-term relevance. When Sai Baba had called me 'Bhakta', it solved a puzzle for me. I was always trying to find out how I could adjust my attitude so that I would gain better interaction with the Truth of a higher dimension, but I was not interested in being a medium. To be called 'Bhakta' was a clue as to the path that I may already be on. Bhakti yoga is the practice of divine love within. These methods are not restricted to any religion, and I could be illiterate and non-denominational and be practising bhakti yoga.

I had been aware when I was in Sai Baba's presence that he was, of course, a man, just like me. That he had 'yogic' powers had been obvious. Therefore, what he said was more believable.

A symbolic divine eye

I attended a talk for Westerners by an elderly Muslim author who spoke about a book that he had written, *Divinity is One*. I was tired and tried to stay alert, but getting up at 3 am daily was taking its toll on my concentration, so I closed my eyes to try to focus. I clearly saw a blue sky and several white cumulus clouds. To my surprise, taking up about half of the 'frame' of my inner vision, there appeared a basic pencil-like sketch of an eye superimposed over the sky scene. I immediately thought, 'That looks like a sketch.' The pupil of the eye moved to its right. I was incredulous. The pupil immediately turned again to move to the front.

When the author had finished his talk, I approached him and told him about my vision. He did not appear to be surprised; he gave the impression that he truly knew what he had been talking about because he quickly responded: 'An eye always represents divinity.'

That evening, I sat in a park. When I looked up at the clear sky, I temporarily saw the outline of several human heads several times over a few minutes. I have never understood why, but this day was probably the first time I had seen a vision when I was not consciously mediating. Over the years since, I have seen numerous visions, particularly when I am drowsy. They have appeared more regularly over the last seven years since I saw a vision of a small, red-covered book, which I understood to be a prompt for me to start to write about the incredible experiences that I have related here now. The eye vision must have been the early beginnings of the 'in body' meditations that Peter had told me Sai Baba recommends.

I had been asked by Indian friends in New Zealand to purchase a book for them in India that was not available in New Zealand at that time. The American author's name was Jack Hawley, a motivational speaker. He had compiled a book from an assortment of about 30 original translations and commentaries that he had named *A Walkthrough for Westerners*. It was Jack's interpretation of the famous Indian spiritual classic, *The Bhagavad Gita*. One English translation of that title is named *The Celestial Song*. Jack had translated the story into modern conversational English to make it accessible and meaningful to more Western people. One day I saw that the sign outside the hall advertising 'Talks for Westerners' was promoting Jack as the speaker. I was an hour too late — I had forgotten to come for that day's talk.

I went up the entrance stairs into the apparently empty hall, but there was an elderly man there who suggested that I check directly downstairs in the North Indian restaurant: 'You might find Jack Hawley there having lunch,' he told me. I did not know what Jack looked like, but I saw the man who always sat next to me when I attended the evening discussion group for Westerners. He always listened attentively to every speaker, and often hurriedly jotted down copious notes as if he had been inspired by something that the speaker said. He was seated at a table with another man.

'Excuse me, do you happen to know a man called Jack Hawley?' I asked.

'I'm the man that you're looking for,' the man genially told me. I could hardly believe my luck. He told me where to purchase a copy of his book, and the next day he graciously signed it for me. I returned to the bookshop and bought a copy for myself.

About two years later, back in New Zealand, I dreamed that I was standing behind a scattering of people on the side of a street, when Sai Baba approached accompanied by several people. They passed by in front of me; it seemed that Sai Baba glanced at me. He has said in the past that no one can dream about him unless he has willed it. However, I did not speak with him in person again.

In October 2019, I was surprised to see Sai Baba in a crystal-clear vision. He appeared to be about 30 years old, as he walked from my left to the right from a straight, tree-lined road that was at right angles to me. He was about four metres from me. Sai Baba was dressed in his usual orange gown and looked very relaxed. He did not look in my direction.

Village life outside the ashram

During my final days in India, I went outside the ashram walls after morning darshan and looked around the village. Directly outside the ashram entrance there was always a row of women in colourful saris, sitting shoulder to shoulder at their market tables selling locally grown fresh fruit and fresh flower garlands.

There was a European-style restaurant in the village, and it did a brisk business; they had the option of meat meals on the menu. Some of the other restaurants in the village had grubby furniture so I ate my meals in the ashram, usually at the Westerners' restaurant, which was staffed by volunteers. A Sanskrit grace followed by an English translation was always chanted by everyone present before the food was served. The words displayed on a blackboard acknowledged that God had provided the food.

A film-developing shop in the village always had a steady flow of customers. There were many tiny typical Asian shops. I observed several two-storeyed apartment blocks, and new ones were being constructed.

Some retailers had their wares stacked up to the edge of the footpath. I was walking in the village one day when a stunningly beautiful woman about 22 years old, carrying a grubby baby that looked distressed, spoke to me in perfect English: 'Sir, will you give money for the baby?' I had read warnings about beggars who carry suffering children for sympathy but who are not poor, so I decided to be kind but practical. 'Don't give money,' my father had told me when I was a youth. 'Buy a meal and give that to them.' He had probably been referring to alcoholics. Another young woman with a baby hovered close by, looking desperate, and then other beggars quickly surrounded me, one a young man walking on his hands that he placed between his useless legs.

'Hello, sir!' he said as he flashed a huge cheery smile.

The first woman could see that I was hesitating. 'Buy milk for the baby then, sir.' She gazed at me intently.

I agreed to buy her some milk, but as I stood in front of the nearby shop the gathering crowd worried the shopkeeper, who picked up a thick wooden staff and threatened the beggars who were brushing up against the stock displayed close to the street. He looked worried and scowled as he produced a packet of powdered milk to show me. I asked for two packets, and then placed one of them under my left arm when he handed them to me. It was immediately removed by someone behind me as I fumbled to find the correct money to pay the shopkeeper. I glanced around and saw a barefooted young girl about eight years old in a dishevelled plain white cotton dress walking off determinedly with the packet of milk. She did not look back. I thought that she had showed admirable initiative for her age, so I could not be angry. I ordered an extra packet, paid the shopkeeper and handed one packet to each of the two women with a baby and then quickly made my way past all the people gathered around.

If I was alone, it was prudent to walk steadily along at a good pace so that beggars were not encouraged to intervene. Sai Baba has said that visitors to the ashram were on a spiritual journey for themselves and should leave the beggar problem to him. He said that visitors did not travel a long way to get here to worry about other people's problems.

There was a large notice in the ashram reception area advising that it was unwise to give locals any gifts because it caused jealousy in the village. There should not be any beggars because the locals were taken care of by the Sai Baba Trust. I was told that beggars arrived from other regions to take advantage of the many visitors to the ashram for Sai Baba's upcoming birthday celebrations. Apparently, he had no wish for a celebration, but allowed it to keep his devotees happy.

Sai Baba distributed free saris to the local women at certain times of the year, according to the available information. The Sai Baba Trust had constructed water wells for 800 villages in the region around his ashram at huge cost. Sai Baba had refused to personally own any property.

On one occasion I waited in a queue behind an elderly man that I had often seen accompanying Sai Baba. He told me that he was a doctor and was part of a medical team that went around the villages with Sai Baba between darshans. Another man sitting beside me one morning at darshan told me that he was a doctor at one of the hospitals. With tears in his eyes, he told me that Sai Baba worked long hours every day and would not take rests despite his age.

The Trust also ran a free primary school, university, music conservatory and museum. I visited the beautiful international-standard Super Specialty Hospital that I had seen being constructed on the video I had watched in New Zealand. The magnificent hospital was scrupulously clean, which was gratifying to see after the apparent lack of hygiene in some other premises in the village. There is also a small general hospital in Puttaparthi. I learned that there are Sai Baba hospitals and education centres in other cities. There is no charge for treatment. A booklet informed that a donation may be given to the Trust but is not asked for.

My final days in India

At darshan, Sai Baba now had an extra youth following him with a bag to carry the increasing number of letters being collected. I had been at the ashram for almost two weeks. Buses were arriving more frequently because Sai Baba's birthday was about 10 days away and many people were preparing for the celebration. Up until now I had not seen any outward show of prosperity by any devotee but there were now a few women wearing expensive silk saris.

I left the ashram with the same people I had arrived with. I had not seen them during my time there. They told me that they had been directly behind me when Sai Baba invited me for an audience with him and were excited to hear what had transpired during my interview with him. The leader of the group and his charges had also had an interview. Interviews were able to be arranged for some Western travellers from spiritual organisations. The leader told me that Sai Baba had encouraged him not to return to this ashram again, but instead travel to the Himalayas on his next trip. They had already arranged to travel to the Himalayas as part of their current itinerary.

The tour leader discovered that his sandals had disappeared. 'It is the third pair that has gone missing since we arrived,' he said. Each time devotees entered a building, not including retail shops, it was the custom that footwear be left outside. Thousands of sandals would be piled up in the alleyways around the mandir entrances every time the devotees entered for darshan. I had taken the precaution of sticking a wide, bright-yellow tape with a black stripe around my sandals and bag before I left New Zealand. This made it easier to locate the luggage at the airports and my footwear among the piles of sandals outside the ashram buildings. The presence of the coloured tape must have helped to discourage anyone from taking my possessions. The tour leader had to hobble along without his footwear.

There were a few minutes of panic; because of the extra birthday traffic and hundreds of extra pedestrians milling around outside the ashram, how would we find the vehicle that had been sent by the travel agent? We had to return to Bangalore, and I had to connect with my flight to leave the country. Somehow the young man waiting to transport us saw us and took us to his vehicle.

The return trip to Bangalore and New Zealand was uneventful.

Chapter 14
Back in New Zealand

Back in New Zealand I was asked to give a talk to Sai Baba devotees at the usual Thursday evening bhajans. They listened attentively as I told them what had transpired for me at Sai Baba's ashram. For two or three years after my interview, whenever I talked about my experiences in India, I had to struggle to control my emotions, or I would feel like a bubble was about to burst and I would be in tears again. It is difficult to explain the heartfelt joy of knowing that there is a spiritual aspect to life that affects the mind and body. As the years passed, I realised that there must have been unseen emanations from the temple area that had instigated the electrical or magnetic activity in my body.

My White Eagle group of friends were thrilled that I had had an interview with Sai Baba. 'I'm so pleased for you,' was Marie's response. I gave her some of the vibhuti that I had been given by Sai Baba. A few weeks later she told me she had been suffering from some illness and was advised by Sai Baba to take a teaspoon of vibhuti with water twice a day. She had regained her health.

By chance I saw the woman that I had spoken to before going to India — the woman who operated an aura camera. She told me that she 'saw' that I was leaning against a rock on a beach. 'The worst is behind you,' she said. Mark, my clairvoyant friend, said that he would be interested to see an aura photograph of me that has been taken since meeting Sai Baba. By an incredible coincidence, the same aura camera operator who had taken all my previous photographs was working his camera at an annual 'lifestyle' fair that was nearby. The fair was about to close. I hurried there and was just in time to get an aura photograph taken. I was happy to show Mark that in the resulting photograph my aura colours indicated that I was now totally stress-free. Had the three 'zaps' that I had received at Sai Baba's ashram released my tensions? I may never know, but my friend was impressed with my newest photograph because he had seen the one taken immediately before I left for India.

While shopping I saw a woman that had been accompanying the woman at the marae who had told me that I would meet Sai Baba about 12 months previously. She was pleased to hear confirmation that I had received the money predicted and met Sai Baba. This meeting was another coincidence because I was in Hamilton, 20 kilometres from where I had been given the message.

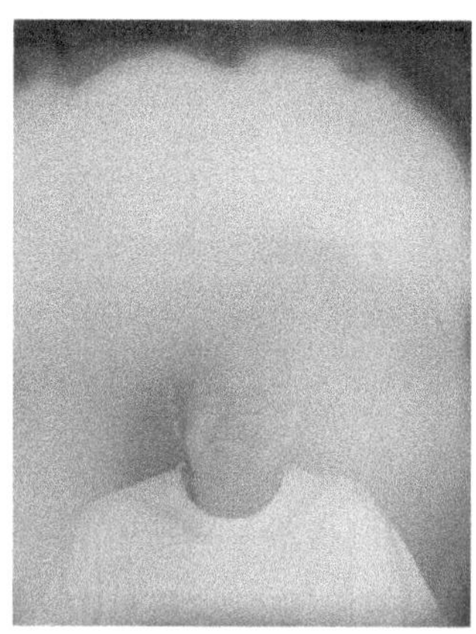

The author after visiting Sai Baba, 2001

Another coincidence?

I thought I might be able to do some study at home that could help me to qualify for a job that I was already partly experienced for. It would involve a change from my most recent occupations. I had been the owner of restaurants for 15 years and had then spent five years as an employee manufacturing boutique ice cream. However, when I was younger, I had spent two years in Sydney as a KFC manager and afterwards spent two years as a driving instructor. Before I had travelled to India my friend Mark had said to me: 'I know that you had been a driving instructor when you were young; would you please give my four children driving lessons?' I agreed and spent the next few months training them. That is how I got to realise that there may occasionally be employment opportunities as a driving licence testing officer. On a whim, I made a telephone enquiry and was surprised that there was a training course commencing soon. 'Did you see our advertisement?' asked the training manager that I spoke to. No, I had not — I had merely been intending to make preliminary enquiries. The manager told me that he was interviewing applicants as we spoke! An appointment to meet him was arranged for the next day, after which I was accepted to commence a training course starting in a few weeks' time. I was 'lucky' again! The messages about 'a job coming up' and 'giving a different type of reading' were coming to fruition. I had also been told, 'You are going to be busy!' Marie had told me that she had seen a golden road ahead for me, and Phyllis Tantrum had said that an interesting time was coming up at the end of 2001. These predictions were to come true.

I passed my examinations and started work. When I was unsure whether my work was satisfactory, I was reassured by a brief phrase from White Eagle through Marie that I 'was doing all right'. I took perhaps 22,000 applicants for an individual on-road driving test over the following nine years. For more than seven years I had never been involved in an accident while a driving licence applicant was driving. However, over the last two years of my testing days, two drivers made sudden errors that were impossible to prevent. The cars involved were both write-offs but there were no serious injuries. I had received two visions and a dream warning me months earlier. I enjoyed the work but during the previous few months I had been plagued by a feeling of dread. I could not understand why. I felt reasonably well except for stiff muscles in my legs. However, I had to undergo an urgent heart bypass surgery because of a sudden blood vessel blockage. This may have been affecting me mentally and caused my body to send warning signals. I had been regularly waking up during the night for no apparent reason for several months. I slept soundly after I recovered from the operation and my depressive feelings were replaced by calm.

Should I feel gratitude to Sathya Sai Baba for clearing the way for me? Can I really put my trust in a guru? However, nothing can be achieved without first trying — and having faith: a firm belief without logical proof, which should be confirmed by intelligent study. This attitude must have contributed to my psychic and spiritual advancement, but I know that no advancement could have been achieved if I had not developed individual, persistent effort. This is something that you cannot be gifted.

Afterword

The mystical experiences that I have written about were just a start to having 'instant' visions more frequently. Sometimes the dreams and visions are indicative of future events; sometimes they appear to be a symbolic message, but often there is no obvious reason why I am presented with them. I strive to keep every thought positive.

My childhood hope, that I would find a person like Jesus or the Buddha alive in the world today who teaches people how they could become genuinely human, and live to their full potential, was realised. A sympathetic magnetism had to be established between the 'devotee' — me — and the chosen master — Sathya Sai Baba. What I had read years previously, that a master — a person adept at harmonising with nature — will always respond to a determined seeker, had proved to be true.

I would urge the reader to try to avoid stubbornly prejudiced acquaintances or organisations. Do not expect to see visible evidence of spiritual advancement although it will be happening because of your determined effort.

Final words

> 'We are blessed or condemned by our own actions.' — Sathya Sai Baba. *Seva*.

There are no miracles. Kriya yoga or kriya shakti are the means by how so-called miracles are produced. Only an adept or an advanced disciple has the qualities necessary to do so. The imagination constructs a model of what is desired and then the willpower is engaged. The adept utilises and manipulates nature's materials. You have read how I witnessed these incidences when I was within one metre of Sathya Sai Baba.

Recommended reading

THESE BOOKS OR THEIR LATER EDITIONS ARE available at public libraries or online, and give explanations about chakras, auras and meditations, and information about spiritual development.

The Theosophical Society brought to Western countries the awareness of Eastern spiritual knowledge. Available in their libraries, *The Mahatma Letters to A.P. Sinnett* contains an incredible record of correspondence between spiritual adepts — masters — in India and a famous newspaper editor in the nineteenth century.

Available to purchase or borrow from the Theosophical Society: *The Occult World,* and *Esoteric Buddhism.* Summarising esoteric information — old but informative.

Unbelievable by Stacy Horn, 2009, HarperCollins, New York, US. This book details information about the scientific investigations conducted by Duke University into 'ghosts, poltergeists, telepathy and other unseen phenomena'.

Man's Eternal Quest by Paramahansa Yogananda, 1975, Self-Realization Fellowship, California, US. This book has comparative deep spiritual meanings of Indian and Christian scriptures. It contains inspiring in-depth, practical guidance for self-development.

Autobiography of a Yogi by Paramahansa Yogananda, 1946, The Philosophical Library, New York, US. About the author's enthusiastic meetings with gurus while searching for his own personal guru. A classic.

About the Author

David's varied career has seen him running coffee bars, KFCs, a chain of pizza stores which he owned and sold, and co-owning an Italian restaurant, before becoming a driving licence testing officer which he did until his retirement. A fascinating chapter of his early career was his membership of a controversial 'utopian' society that owned Rakino Island in Auckland's Hauraki Gulf where he lived and worked for several years. David is now retired. He has one married son and two grandchildren and lives in Auckland, New Zealand.

Contact David: eternal.swan.publishing@gmail.com

Acknowledgments

I am grateful to have had crucial editorial advice with early drafts from Keith Hill, who pointed out structural errors and suggested other improvements.

www.ingramcontent.com/pod-product-compliance
Ingram Content Group UK Ltd.
Pitfield, Milton Keynes, MK11 3LW, UK
UKHW020132250726
13967UKWH00002B/610

9 780473 625771